CAN YOU TEACH

Anna Craft

with

Jana Dugal
Gordon Dyer
Bob Jeffrey
Tom Lyons

Published 1997 by Education Now Publishing Co-operative
113 Arundel Drive, Bramcote Hills, Nottingham NG9 3FQ

British Library Cataloguing in Publication Data

Craft, Anna

CAN YOU TEACH CREATIVITY?
1. Title

ISBN 1 871526 25 6

Cover illustrations: Natasha Hyman and Holly Clarke

Design and production: JSB for Education Now Books

Printed in Great Britain by
Antony Rowe Ltd, Chippenham, Wiltshire

Contents

Preface
About the authors

Part 1: "Does it mean being theatrical?"
What creativity is, and what it is not

Part 2: Fostering creativity across the curriculum

Part 3: Teachers developing their practice

Part 4: Vision

Postscript: Humane Creativity in the Classroom

Preface

This book has been written in the belief that the fostering of creativity, in educators and children, is critical for constructive social development.

Part 1 explores a variety of aspects of creativity. In Chapter 1, I discuss creativity as a way of life, exploring 'possibility thinking', the notion of 'intelligences', characteristics of the creating mind, and what creativity might look like in the classroom. In Chapter 2, I introduce a framework for conceptualising and analysing creativity in education, through a case study of two children whom I know well.

Part 2 focuses on the school curriculum and explores the extent to which creativity is both manifest and fostered in different school subjects. Working from the premise that creativity is central to all subjects, Chapter 3 explores creativity in the performing, expressive and visual arts, and also the humanities. In Chapter 4 the focus shifts to mathematics, science, information technology and design and technology. Chapters 3 and 4 draw on case studies of children and teachers across the 3 - 13 age range.

Part 3 looks at various aspects of teachers developing their pedagogy. In Chapter 5, Bob Jeffrey suggests a methodology for classroom teachers to identify and develop their practice in fostering children's creativity, exemplifying this through a case study. He draws on the case study to suggest a number of frames through which creative teaching might be described. In Chapter 6, I widen the discussion to consider the impact of culture on characteristics of pedagogy and pupil creativity, drawing on a collaborative research project which I am engaged in with colleagues in Southern Spain. The chapter closes with a revisiting of teacher artistry. In Chapter 7, Tom Lyons and I explore ways in which the educator can be nourished, in order to foster creativity in learners. Drawing on our research project, we suggest a range of practical strategies.

Part 4 looks at vision in education, exploring the practicalities of developing and manifesting it. In Chapter 8, Gordon Dyer and I introduce social systems thinking, and explore its application within the school. Chapter 9, written with Jana Dugal, explores barriers and challenges to vision, from the personal to the social.

I would like to thank all the learners and teachers with whom I have worked over the years, and who have collectively inspired the writing of this book. I hope that they may recognise themselves in it. Thank you also to Natasha Hyman, my four-and-a-half-year-old niece, and ten-year-old Holly Clarke, for their cover illustrations, and Roland and Janet Meighan and John and Iram Siraj-Blatchford at *Education Now,* for their encouragement and support in bringing the book to fruition; particularly to John for his helpful comments on the text. Heartfelt thanks are due also to my parents, Maurice and Alma Craft for their close reading of the final draft and for teaching me the importance of answering one question by asking another; one of the foundations of the creative disposition. Finally, but by no means least, I am eternally grateful to Simon, my partner, for his continual inspiration and support.

Anna Craft
London, April 1997

About the Authors

Anna Craft is a Lecturer in primary education and teacher development at The Open University, having taught infants and junior aged children in Inner London. She formerly worked at the University of North London and then at the National Curriculum Council on projects in economic awareness. Her current research focus is creativity in education. She founded and convenes a UK-wide seminar network on creativity in education, which meets monthly in London. She is an Associate Director of *Education Now,* a member of the Scientific and Medical Network and of the Creative Education Foundation. Her most recent book is *Continuing Professional Development* (Routledge, 1996).

Jana Dugal is Director of The Institute for Creativity, leading workshop processes developed to initiate and propose creativity as a way of experiential living. Co-author of the Institute's postgraduate course, *Creativity in Education,* accredited by The Open University, she tutors the course and has since 1995 worked with educators and managers in schools to initiate vision. Composer and voice coach, Jana has taught singing and voice development work in the UK and USA music industry. Her opera, The Voice Circus, is a music resource designed for Key Stages 2 and 3. She runs educator courses on creativity, some of which combine holiday with professional development, across Europe.

Gordon Dyer is tenured as a Senior Lecturer in the Faculty of Technology at the Open University. He is currently Deputy Director of the East Anglian Region, an appointment he has held since 1985. Prior to joining the OU he served for 26 years in the RAF where he held a variety of operational flying, training and staff appointments. Over the years, his interest and research in systems has moved in emphasis from those of a technical kind to social systems. He is an active member of the International Systems Institute (ISI) and is Chair of its Transcultural Council. The work within the ISI is much involved in the issue of the requirements for systems of human development and learning which will enable future generations to design better lives for themselves.

Bob Jeffrey is a Research Fellow in the School of Education at The Open University. Formerly, he taught in London primary schools for over twenty years. He has an MA in Education Management and is currently working on a PhD focusing on the intensification of primary teachers' work. Recently he and Peter Woods completed a study of creative teaching, which resulted in the book *Teachable Moments: The Art of Teaching in Primary Schools* and a number of articles. He is currently researching the effects of Ofsted inspections on primary teachers and their work and hopes to begin a new research project with Peter Woods developing the idea of creative learning in the primary school based mainly on pupil perspectives.

Tom Lyons is an education consultant. He works for the Open University both as an Assistant Staff Tutor and a course tutor where he has taught on the postgraduate modules *Evaluating and Planning Professional Development* and more recently *Creativity in Education* which, additionally he co-researched with Anna Craft. He also works as an Associate Lecturer in the School of Education at Brunel University. He taught in secondary schools for seventeen years before going on to manage two Teachers Centres in Huntingdon and more recently in Harrow. He was also responsible for the co-ordination of teacher in-service education and training in the London borough of Harrow with whom he continues to be involved as the chair of governors of a first and middle school. He is co-author of *Professional Development Portfolios.*

Part 1

'Does it mean being theatrical?'

What creativity is, and what it is not

Introduction

The question about creativity which I am asked most frequently by educators, concerns what meaning of the word itself. The idea that creativity is somehow to do with the creative arts, with the theatre, with 'being arty,' is widely prevalent in my experience. But this is not the whole story!

The two chapters in Part One explore aspects of what creativity really is. In the first chapter, I explore the notion of 'possibility thinking' and trawl some existing definitions of creativity, applying these to education. In Chapter 2, I offer a practical framework for understanding and fostering children's creativity across the curriculum.

In this way I hope that Part One will start to open up thinking on what creativity means in the curriculum of children aged 3 to 13. I hope it will provide practical suggestions for how teachers could develop their practice to foster it.

Anna Craft

Chapter 1

Possibility Thinking and 'What if?'

Anna Craft

*In this chapter, I first explore creative action
as a way of life and discuss possibility
thinking as core to creativity. I explore the
notion, introduced by Howard Gardner, of
'multiple intelligences', and also the notion
of qualities involved in the 'creating mind'.
Finally, I ask what creativity might look like
in the classroom for children aged 3 - 13, and
for the teachers who work with them.*

Possibility thinking

Picture an experienced teacher working with children aged 8 - 13 in one of the middle schools in a small town in the heart of England.

Anji, an experienced teacher, has co-ordinated information technology in the school for the past ten years. She has created an IT resource and teaching room which serves all of the five hundred children in the school, finding ways of cobbling together a wide variety of machines including some which still use audio-cassettes instead of floppy disks. She is a convert to the possibilities which information technology offers to children and adults, although she has an uphill struggle in convincing some of her colleagues of this. The resource room is in a one-storey part of the school which has a flat roof and during the winters it often leaks, so that she has to pull the apparatus away from the walls and some of the computers have to be disconnected from the network. She regularly writes programmes which will meet the needs of the specific children whom she is teaching. She is passionate about her subject, sets very high standards for the children and is highly regarded by children and parents alike. Above

all, she will never let a problem which has arisen, block a child's learning. Consequently, she is often to be seen in the resource room during breaks, after school and at weekends, puzzling over software and hardware problems, and sometimes, during wet lunchtimes and playtimes, helping children to learn.

Anji is a teacher who uses 'possibility thinking' as a fundamental perspective in her own professional life. She aims consciously to foster it in the children she teaches in her choice of computer software and activities. So what does it mean?

For me, possibility thinking means two things. First, it means not being stumped by one set of circumstances, but using imagination to find a way around a problem. Second, it is about asking questions. As Professor Philip Gammage has suggested, education should not be about 'answering the question', but rather about 'questioning the answer'. And possibility thinking is about posing lots of questions. Children enter school doing this naturally, as John Holt has said (1991):

> 'The easily observable fact is that children are passionately eager to make as much sense as they can of the world around them, are extremely good at it, and do as scientists do, by creating knowledge out of experience. Children observe, wonder, find, or make and then test the answers to the questions they ask themselves. When they are not actually prevented from doing these things, they continue to do them and to get better and better at it.'
>
> (Holt, 1991, p152)

Possibilities through play

Playing is an important part of possibility thinking. According to Hudson (1973), Einstein himself considered 'combinatory play' to be a key part of his own creative thinking. And play forms a part of the six areas of learning (one of which is called 'Creative

Development'), which nursery schools now have to provide for children (OFSTED, 1996). Among those who research creativity in the arts there has long been a fascination about the relationship between the child and the artist, as Gardner has documented (1994).

There is some evidence that children who have plenty of play experiences which invoke non-standardised responses (eg dramatic play, or engaging with non-structured and also multi-purpose play objects) are more readily creative on other tasks (Pepler, 1982). So, play which has a strong imitative, intellectual, convergent or neutral 'flavour' seems to foster less creativity than experimental play, or what I call 'possibility playing'. There is also some evidence that social play is more conducive to creativity than solitary play, and that adult intervention to stimulate imagination helps. (Pepler, ibid). Dansky (1980) has shown that children who are highly predisposed toward fantasy in play are more likely to be imaginative in a task situation - and that some children are more predisposed toward fantasy play than others. Some practical implications for schools of this research on play are:

* that possibility thinking is not just for adults;

* that children need opportunities and models for playing together and independently throughout the school day;

* that time needs to be allowed for children to do this;

* that possibility thinking is not just about what happens in lessons; playtimes and the playground and dinner halls also provide rich potential for supporting it;

* that some children will find it easier than others to engage with possibility thinking or possibility play.

A creative teacher will stimulate and support

possibility thinking in a variety of ways and across the curriculum. These will include playing through, for example:

* puppetry
* dramatic play
* role play
* open-ended scenarios
* improvisation
* empathy work
* simulations
* fantasy modelling
* story telling.

Some activities will be deliberately structured, and others much less so. For example, drama improvisation in pairs may be set up quite deliberately in a way that free play in the home corner is not.

Possibility in divergent and convergent thinking

The earlier work of Liam Hudson (1973) suggested that children who excel in science, maths, technology, are also children who do well on traditional IQ tests, where there is one right answer. In other words, they are good at convergent thinking, where there is just one solution to the problem. On the other hand, those children who are divergent thinkers, finding several possibilities for each question, tend to excel in the arts. In other words, they are good at thinking of many possible solutions to a problem. Hudson's thesis was that the arts and the sciences demand different kinds of thinking. One implication of his view is that science, maths and technology are uncreative, in that they involve a very focused perspective on possibility thinking.

In this book I take a different view. I would argue that possibility thinking, which is the basis of creativity, is involved in both convergent and divergent thinking - a position which John White, philosopher of education, has started to map out (1972). In chapters 2, 3 and 4, I try to show how, for me, possibility thinking is at the core of creativity.

Possibility thinking as the core of creativity

The Pocket Oxford English Dictionary describes creativity as:

'bringing into existence, giving rise to, originating, being imaginative and inventive'.
(6th Edition, 1978)

So the word creativity describes flux, change, development, growth. It describes the approach to life which begins with: **'perhaps if'...** or **'what if'.....** and I characterise this questioning core of creativity as "possibility thinking". I would include in this the possibility thinking of which we are not necessarily conscious.

Possibility and self-actualisation

There is a sense in which creativity involves making out of nothing. And, of course, there are different theoretical perspectives on this phenomenon. For example, *Freudian psychology* which might define creativity as the sublimation of a sexual urge, or *Skinnerian psychology* which might describe creativity as simply the revealing of pre-existent ideas, rather than conjuring them up. Or the *information processing perspectives* which equate the brain to a computer, and might construct creativity in terms of searching the long-term memory for appropriate solutions to a problem.

Or *humanistic psychology*, based on Maslow's ideas (1971) which sees creativity as self-actualization and a special talent to boot. I return to Maslow's ideas and humanistic psychology in Chapter 3. There is the *psychosynthetic perspective* which sees creativity as involving conscious choice over levels of unconscious processes. These are only some of the perspectives which can be found in one field - psychology. Other fields, such as sociology, philosophy, spirituality, studies in education, yield further definitions.

My own approach draws more upon psychosynthesis and humanistic psychology, partly because I think they have particular relevance to classroom teaching. I therefore see creativity as being to do with self-

actualisation, and involving choice, which is informed by levels of unconscious processes. Later in this book, in chapter 2, I will explore these notions further.

Summing up so far:

I have introduced possibility thinking as a core element in creativity and have suggested that it involves:

* play
* asking questions
* not allowing problems or circumstances to block action

I have suggested possibility thinking is involved in both convergent and divergent thinking. Having discussed briefly some of the perspectives through which creativity can be viewed, I have introduced the notion of creativity as enabling the individual to achieve self-actualisation. This notion comes from the tradition of psychosynthesis and humanistic psychology.

The next part of this chapter examines the idea of creativity as "multiple intelligence".

Creativity and intelligence

Creativity is not the same as intelligence, in the sense of IQ, as research from the 1970s and 1980s has shown (Wallach, 1971, 1985). Also, we now know that certain kinds of divergent thinking skills can be improved with practice and training. But perhaps the most useful breakthrough in understanding creativity which has occurred in the past twenty years is the notion of creativity as multiple intelligence.

Multiple intelligences

In the mid 1980s, Howard Gardner, a leading researcher exploring creativity at Harvard University, put forward a pluralist theory of mind which aimed to recognise the different cognitive styles and strengths of individuals. He called it the 'theory of multiple intelligences' (1984, 1993). Initially, he put forward seven intelligences as follows:

Linguistic intelligence: facility with language.

Logical-mathematical intelligence: ability in logical, mathematical and scientific thinking. Gardner claims that Piaget, the influential developmental psychologist, whilst claiming to be studying the development of all intelligence (including moral development), was in fact studying only this form.

He also notes that 'if you do well in language and logic, you should do well in IQ tests and SATS [Standard Assessment Tasks - ie national tests in England and Wales for children aged 7 and 11], and you may well get into a prestigious college' (1993, p8) but then argues that what happens to you once you leave full time education depends on 'the extent to which you possess and use the other intelligences' (ibid, p8 - 9). These he initally named as:

Spatial intelligence: facility with forming a manoeuvrable and operational mental model of the spatial world. Surgeons, painters, sailors, engineers are all examples of professions involving spatial intelligence.

Musical intelligence: facility with music and sound. Performers, composers, conductors, require this kind of intelligence.

Bodily-kinaesthetic intelligence: ability in solving problems or creating products using the whole body, or parts of it. Athletes, craftspeople and dancers for example all utilise bodily-kinaesthetic intelligence.

Interpersonal intelligence: ability to understand and relate to other people. Successful politicians, teachers, salespeople all have this kind of intelligence.

Intrapersonal intelligence: capacity to understand oneself accurately and to apply that understanding effectively in life.

He is currently working on a further intelligence or more, thus his current thinking is sometimes referred to as 'eight and a half intelligences'. He suggests

(1996) that *Naturalist intelligence* may be a further one, as may *Spiritual* and *Existential* intelligences, which he is less sure about. By *Naturalist intelligence,* he means capability and expertise in recognising and classifying the flora and fauna of numerous species. I would argue that 'non-conscious' intelligence, should be added to his original seven, as a part of the wider 'spiritual intelligence'. This I explain further in Chapter 2.

The idea of there being many capabilities of which we each possess different combinations, is not new, nor is it the only one. Charles Handy, the management guru, for example, has proposed nine different forms of intelligence: factual, analytical, linguistic, spatial, musical, practical, physical, intuitive and interpersonal (1994). And, from the adult learning field, the various different approaches to 'learning style' also acknowledge different cognitive strengths in individuals (for example, Honey and Mumford, 1986).

The point which is relevant for me in the various formulations of multiple intelligence, is that if the process of 'possibility thinking' is at the core of creativity, what Gardner, Handy and Honey and Mumford do is to open up the applications of possibility thinking.

Howard Gardner's notion of multiple intelligences is widely debated, and the theory has its critics. However, as an attempt to acknowledge the breadth of human capability in a very practical way I find it a useful framework, because it has implications for the way we teach in schools. Clearly, the emphasis through statutory curriculum and assessment arrangements is on linguistic and logical-mathematical intelligences. But to develop each child's capabilities appropriately, we need to broaden our own awareness of the intelligences which we can foster, and in which different individuals may be strong. Consequently in fostering creativity in schools, we need to be more geared toward individuals, their passions and their capabilities.

Consider this case study from a classroom of nine and ten year-old children in North London.

The children were invited to participate in a 'passion assembly' - in other words, to create something to represent what they are passionate about. A nine year old girl wrote a 4000 word story about cruelty to animals. It was really a short novel. An identifiable achievement, it was rightly praised and validated by her teacher and by the head teacher in the school. But her friend's passion is for cooking. His pride in his achievement in creating a sponge cake in the shape of his favourite food, pasta, was not given the same esteem and recognition as his friend's story.

Why not?

My point is that educating for creativity must involve acknowledging all of the different ways in which children are able to exercise possibility thinking. In Chapter 2, I consider the relationship between domains of knowledge and creativity, which is an extension of this idea.

Summing up on creativity as multiple intelligence:

Having explored some aspects of possibility thinking, I have briefly acknowledged the distinction between creativity and 'intelligence' as a global concept. I went on to look at the notion of creativity in education involving the fostering of children's possibility thinking in a variety of domains and forms. In doing so, I have introduced an application of possibility thinking in Howard Gardner's 'multiple intelligence' theory as one highly developed approach.

The next part of this chapter looks at characteristics of the mind which are disposed to possibility thinking, or what I shall call 'the creating mind'.

The creating mind

Many people have written about the core qualities of the creative mind, or what I will call, as Howard Gardner does, 'the creating mind' - a phrase which embodies some of the dynamism and 'flow' involved. In Chapter 2, I will be exploring some of the 'essentialist' personality and biographical factors which Howard Gardner (1993b) has identified in a range of 'unambiguous cases' of creating minds. But for now, I want to concentrate on some of the characteristics of mature, highly creating minds, as documented by others (MacKinnon, 1962, 1978; and Barron, 1969). Based on research studies, they suggest that mature, highly creative people:

* seek to open their minds and those of others to the new;
* think for themselves;
* spend long periods of time seeking to integrate their own thinking with what is outside of them;
* seek resolution by sustained 'to-ing and fro-ing' from within to outside themselves.

So, curiosity and sustained openness to integrating thinking with experience is key to successful creators. Many studies have been conducted, mainly in the USA, on characteristics which are associated with creativity. Some of the most commonly identified traits, collated by Shallcross (1981), for example, are:

openness to experience
independence
self-confidence
willingness to risk
sense of humour or playfulness
enjoyment of experimentation
sensitivity
lack of a feeling of being threatened
personal courage
unconventionality
flexibility
preference for complexity
goal orientation
internal control
originality
self-reliance
persistence
curiosity
vision
self-assertion

acceptance of disorder
motivation
inclination to the off-beat

Source: Shallcross (1981), p10 - 11

Intrinsic motivation, in other words, the desire to produce ideas or work for its own sake rather than through some form of external pressure, has been shown by Amabile (1983, 1985, 1990) to be characteristic of creative individuals also.

Having the motivation to create implies there may be inner mental conditions for fostering creativity. Carl Rogers (1970) whose thinking has had a large influence in the arena of counselling and therapy, (through his notion of 'person-centred counselling'), identified the following three inner conditions for creativity:

* openness to experience (a concept which he calls 'extensionality');
* an internal locus of evaluation (in relation to oneself);
* ability to toy with elements and concepts (ie the ability to play).

So, we are building a picture of what the core attributes of a creating mind might look like.

I have already noted that much of the personality trait research and thinking on creativity has taken place in the United States. Much of the literature which is drawn upon in this book is either North American or from the UK. It is important to acknowledge the possible 'cultural saturation' of these sources. In other words, what is being described is Western concepts of creativity, which are drawn from studies taken in highly developed economies. It is also possible that what is being described is imbued with class-based assumptions. For example, it could be argued that 'goal orientation' and 'internal control', 'self-reliance', 'persistence' from Shallcross's list are all class-related behaviours (ie middle class). There may be other biases within the models presented, which are to do with cultural context. Later in the book, in Chapter 6, I try to demonstrate the importance of cultural context

through a case study of work I have been doing with teachers in Spain. But for now simply be aware that although the literature cited may be strongly indicative of the creativity phenomenon in any learning situation, but not necessarily indicative- ie it is only a perspective on 'truth'.

Recent brain research has added another dimension to the creating mind: the notion of right and left brain activity, which may also have some relevance, and this is considered below.

The physical location of logic and intuition

Medical research has established over the last thirty years, that the two hemispheres of the brain appear to take on slightly different roles in the development of our capabilities. Although there has been controversy over the extent to which these roles can be simplified (Cline, 1989), nevertheless there are some deeply illuminative aspects of the research which I will attempt to summarise here.

Each hemisphere appears to have its own area of specialization, and processes information in its own way; and, of course, in the normal brain, the two hemispheres communicate with one another through the *corpus collosum,* the mass of nerve fibres which bridges the hemispheres.

For the great majority of the population, it is the left hemisphere which controls logical, linear thinking. This is the side which can compute maths, remembers names, learns to read, memorises. The other hemisphere by contrast is the part of the brain where metaphors are understood, where emotions are felt and where dreams, imageries and fantasy occur. It is thought (Zdenek, 1985) that in Western society which is left-brain dominant, the right-hemisphere does not develop as fully as the left, through under-use. Indeed, initially, doctors called the left hemisphere the dominant one. It seems, however, that the left hemisphere is dominant only for the following tasks:

* verbal
* analytical
* literal

    *   linear, and
    *   mathematical.

The left hemisphere may then be particularly good at 'convergent' thinking - although not exclusively, since verbal tasks may involve finding many possible solutions to a problem, ie 'divergent thinking' . The left hemisphere also controls movement on the opposite side of the body.

The right brain by contrast, appears to be dominant for the following kinds of activity:

    *   non-verbal
    *   holistic (non-linear)
    *   spatial
    *   musical
    *   metaphoric
    *   imaginative
    *   artistic
    *   emotional
    *   sexual
    *   spiritual
    *   dreams.

Like the left hemisphere, the right hemisphere controls movement on the opposite side of the body. It may be that the right hemisphere is particularly good at supporting divergent thinking - and creativity more widely.

This breakdown of responsibility in the brain appears to hold true for around 95% of the population, including almost all right-handed people. Left-handed people appear to have less clearly defined role definition in the hemispheres. In general the hemispheres work in harmony together, although often the right hemisphere is under-utilised. And it is really this point which is important for education and for fostering creativity. The challenge for teachers is how to find ways of fostering creativity which feed the right brain as well as the left, for all children. Exercise 1 and 2 offer two possible ways of setting up a creative writing task for children in a way which feed the left and right brain.

Exercise 1
An exercise in creativity for the left brain

Invent a character who lives in one of these places:

    A sock
    The old pear tree
    The house in the valley

Write a story about something unexpected which happens to your character on the first day of summer.

Exercise 2
An exercise in creativity for the right brain

Invent a character who lives in one of these places:

a sock

the old pear tree

the house in the valley

It is the first day of summer and something unexpected has happened for your character. Tell the story of what happens next, using comic strip format.

The question is to consider how to set up learning activities so that each hemisphere of the brain are stimulated. At times it may be possible to stimulate both hemispheres at once. At other times different learning activities will prioritise one over the other. It is important that all children have access to balanced opportunities.

Summing up on the creating mind:

Many characteristics have been identified by researchers as present in the successful possibility thinker, or the successful 'creating mind', and I have introduced some of those identified by MacKinnon, Barron and Shallcross. They involve background attitudes of curiosity and sustained openness to integrating thinking with experience, and include the tendency to display intrinsic motivation to explore and create. Some writers suggests that these aspects of the creating mind imply that creativity is 'dispositional' - in other words, that to be creative, one must be 'disposed' toward it. I would support this argument although I would also argue that creativity can be fostered and developed.

I have touched on Carl Rogers' inner conditions for fostering creativity, which were:

* openness to experience

* internal locus of evaluation, and

* ability to play.

I went on to look at the physical location of possibility thinking in logic and intuition, drawing on recent brain research on left and right brain function.

In the final part of this chapter I look at teachers and teaching and develop the notion of the creating mind further.

Teachers, the creating mind and classrooms

What do teachers make of the creating mind?

In their study of over 1000 teachers' attitudes toward creativity, Fryer and Collings (1989) found that most teachers in the study saw creativity in terms of 'imagination', 'originality' and 'self-expression'. Only half regarded 'divergence' as relevant to creativity. Convergent thinking was only seen as relevant by 10.2% of the sample - presumably because very few teachers in the study saw 'possibility thinking' as a core process to creativity. Few teachers saw creativity as involving myserious processes (9.1%). Rather more thought unconscious processes were involved (18.1%). About half saw creativity as involving inspiration (46.6%).

As far as pedagogy is concerned, Fryer and Collings found that teachers highly orientated to creativity had a preference for a pupil-oriented approach to teaching (a finding in my own research with Spanish primary teachers (Craft, Shepherd and Pain, 1996). Fryer and Collings identify an underlying value system linked to 'person orientation', particularly for women teachers and for those specialising in the humanities.

What does creativity look like in the classroom?

In a sense the whole of the rest of this book is an attempt to explore what creativity looks like for children aged 3 to 13, and their teachers.

At this point, the start of the book, I want to emphasise that creativity requires commitment to space. Creating space means being conscious of the physical place of your classroom, and ways in which it may foster children's creativity. Classrooms which foster creativity allow mistakes and encourage experimentation, openness and risk-taking. Shallcross (1981) argues that it is important for each child to have sufficient physical space and time in any learning activity, in order to do just this. And this includes our own interventions in children's thinking. As she says: 'Too often we have a tendency to intervene earlier than we should while a student is working something out.... Those early interventions often discourage rather than encourage' (ibid, p. 15).

Giving children space however is not to say that structure is unimportant. I would propose that clear expectations around the nature of learning opportunities are important. I would support the view put forward by the Plowden Committee themselves which advocated child-centred learning approaches, that although 'the sense of personal discovery influences the intensity of a child's experience, the vividness of his memory and the probability of effective transfer of learning.... At the same time it is true that trivial ideas and methods may be 'discovered'...furthermore, time does not allow children to find their way by discovery to all they have to learn'. (Plowden Report, 1967) Dominant learning theories such as Vygotskian social constructivism rather emphasise the importance of 'modelling' and 'scaffolding' children's understandings from what they know to what they do not. What I am suggesting is that space for conversation, interactions which actually seek the child's perspective, is important in fostering children's creativity.

Making space for creativity also means valuing it. It means creating an overt 'mental climate' as Shallcross (ibid) calls it. It includes foster self-worth and self-esteem. The creative teacher values both achievability and relevance of classroom activities for the children. Achievability means setting challenges for the children which are achievable, to build confidence. Earlier writers such as McClelland referred to this as 'achievement motivation' (Rosen *et al*, 1969). Relevance means checking out children's perspectives on their learning activities, particularly now that the curriculum, even for nursery children, is defined externally and some would say imposed on the teacher-pupil relationship. Woods and Jeffrey (1996) in their study of creativity in primary classrooms, describe how the teachers negotiate knowledge which is relevant and meaningful to the children, attempting to negotiate the gap between the public knowledge of the National Curriculum and the personal knowledge of each child.

In a recent in-depth study of children's own attitudes toward being in creative environments involving 140 children in 5 classrooms, Jeffrey and Woods (1997)

discovered four aspects of classroom experience where the children whom they interviewed particularly appreciated their teachers' efforts in respect of:

* responding to children's feelings (including acknowledging the range of the feelings, and also helping children to feel confident);

* engaging the children's interest (including having a sense of humour, making the learning fun, having imaginative ideas and a resourceful approach);

* maintaining the children's own autonomy/ identity (including giving space to children to develop and implement their own ideas - to think for themselves, including being heard during discussions and disputes, and also allowing children to adopt their own preferred styles of working);

* encouraging children's capacity to reflect critically (through encouraging rational analysis, even when it could include criticism of the teacher, and also by role-detachment between 'their total involvement and the ability to reflect and comment upon their involvement' (Jeffrey and Woods, 1997, p31).

The Jeffrey and Woods study draws attention to the need for trust in a creative classroom. The emotional climate of the classroom needs to offer each child personal confidence and security; as Shallcross writes, 'the ground rules are personal guarantees that allow [children] to grow at their own rate, retain the privacy of their work until they are ready to share it, and prize their possible differences' (op cit, p19).

Finally, it is important to consider the resourcing of any activity and of the learning environment. If children are to be encouraged to think independently in any area of the curriculum, they will need easy access to materials including books, the computer/s, atlases, games, construction materials, puzzles, craft materials and so on. They will need to be able at times to work with others, in pairs and in groups, so the classroom space needs to support all of these possibilities.

I would argue, as others have done, that creative teaching is 'good teaching'. Quite simply, teaching is a job which requires and involves fostering, creativity. Ironically perhaps, this is acknowledged within official documentation from Teaching As a Career, (TASC) which was until recently based in the Department for Education (TASC, 1994a, 1994b) but which is now absorbed within the Teacher Training Agency. Those who have written on creativity in education talk about 'creativity as part of normality, as part of everyday actions and ideas' (Halliwell, 1993: 69). Halliwell describes creativity in teaching as being 'inventive flexibility' because no two groups of learners are identical, and because no two days are the same. Underpinning inventive flexibility, she suggests, are anticipation and imagination, backed up by strong organisation and judgement (control over ideas). Creative teaching is, she suggests, consciously monitored. It depends then, on the following qualities:

* a clear sense of need;
* the ability to read a situation;
* the willingness to take risks;
* the ability to monitor and evaluate events (p71).

The notion of having volition is also embedded in Woods' (1990) description of creative teaching as involving ownership, control, relevance and innovation (for both teacher and learner).

Summing up Chapter 1:

In this chapter, I have introduced:

* some characteristics of possibility thinking, arguing that it is core to creating
* the notion of creativity as applied through multiple intelligences
* some distinguishing features of the creating mind
* some aspects of teachers' attitudes toward fostering creativity in the classroom.

I have suggested that teaching which fosters children's possibility thinking, is 'good teaching'.

Your practice and creativity

Questions to ponder:

Consider how far you would agree with the notion of possibility thinking as the core of creativity, and the act of asking 'what if?' across a range of different intelligences.

Consider how you could develop your practice so that children have more opportunities to play.

Choose a curriculum area and your learning goals for a particular part of the coming week. Consider how you could set up the learning experience so that it works both hemispheres of the brain for the children you teach.

How much space do you allow for the aspects of creativity which the Jeffrey and Woods children identified, ie

* *responding to children's feelings,*
* *engaging the children's interest,*
* *maintaining the children's own autonomy/identity, and*
* *encouraging children's capacity for critical reflection?*

References

Amabile, T. (1983), *The Social Psychology of Creativity,* New York: Springer-Verlag

Amabile, T. (1985), 'Motivation and Creativity: Effects of motivational orientation on creative writers', *Journal of Personality and Social Psychology,* 48, 393 - 399

Amabile, T. (1990), 'Within you, without you: The social psychology of creativity, and beyond. In Runco, M. A. and Albert, R. S. (eds), *Theories of Creativity* pp 61 - 91, Newbury Park, CA: Sage Publications

Barron, F. (1989), *Creative Person and Creative Process,* New York: Holt, Rinehart & Winston

Cline, S. (1989), *What Would Happen If I Said Yes?....* New York: D.O.K. Publishers

Craft, A., Shepherd, R., Pain, A. (1996), *Creativity and Pedagogy in Spain*, Unpublished Working Paper, August 1996

Dansky, J. L. (1980), 'Make-believe: a mediator of the relationship between play and associative fluency', *Child Development*, 51, 576 - 579

Fryer, M., Collings, J.A. (1991), 'Teachers' views about creativity', *British Journal of Educational Psychology*, 61, pp207-219

Gardner, H. (1984), *Frames of Mind: The Theory of Multiple Intelligences*, London: William Heinemann Ltd

Gardner, H. (1993a), *Multiple Intelligences: the theory in practice*, New York: HarperCollins Inc.

Gardner, H. (1994), *The Arts and Human Development*, New York: HarperCollins Inc.

Gardner, H. (1996), 'Are there additional intelligences? The Case for Naturalist, Spiritual, and Existential Intelligences', to appear in Kane, J. (ed), *Education, Information and Transformation*, Engelwood Cliffs, NJ: Prentice-Hall (forthcoming)

Halliwell, S. 'Teacher creativity and teacher education', in Bridges, D. and Kerry, T. (eds) (1993) *Developing Teachers Professionally*, London and New York: Routledge

Handy, C. (1994), *The Empty Raincoat: Making Sense of the Future*, London: Hutchinson

Holt, J. (1991), *Learning all the time*, Education Now Publishing Co-operative, in association with Lighthouse Books

Honey, P., Mumford, A. (1986), *A Manual of Learning Styles*, Maidenhead: Peter Honey and Alan Mumford

Hudson, L. (1973), *Originality*, London: Oxford University Press

Jeffrey, R., Woods, P. (1997), 'The Relevance of Creative Teaching: Pupils' Views', in Pollard, A., Thiessen, D., Filer, A. (eds) (1997), *Children and their Curriculum: The Perspectives of Primary and Elementary School Children*, London: The Falmer Press

MackKinnon, D.W. 'What Makes a Person Creative?' *Saturday Review*, February 10, 1962

MacKinnon, D.W. (1978), *In Search of Human Effectiveness: Identifying and Developing Creativity*, Buffalo, NY: Creative Education Foundation, and Great Neck, NY: Creative Synergetic Associates 1978

Maslow, A.H. (1971), *The Farther Reaches of Human Nature*, Harmondsworth: Penguin Books Ltd.

Office for Standards in Education (OFSTED), (March, 1996), *Training Course for Registered Nursery Education Inspectors: A Guide for Inspectors*, London: HMSO

Pepler, D.J. (1982), Play and Divergent Thinking, in Pepler, D.J. and Rubin, K.H. (eds) (1982), *The Play of Children: Current theory and research*, London: S.Karger

Rogers, C. R. (1970), Towards a Theory of Creativity, in Vernon, P.E. (ed), *Creativity*, Harmondsworth: Penguin Books Ltd

Rosen, B.C., Crockett, H.T. & Nunn, C..Z. (Eds.) (1969) Achievement in Americaan Society, Schenkman Pub. C.., Cambridge, Mass.

Shallcross, D.J. (1981), *Teaching Creative Behaviour: How to Teach Creativity to Children of All Ages*, Englewood Cliffs, New Jersey: Prentice-Hall

TASC (Teaching as a Career), (1994a), *Secondary Teaching: the challenge and the reward*, London: Department for Education

TASC (Teaching as a Career) (1994b), *My teacher: Training to teach in primary schools*, London: Department for Education

Wallach, M. (1971), The creativity-intelligence distinction. New York: General Learning Press

Wallach, M. (1985), Creativity testing and giftedness. In Horowitz, F. and O'Brien, M. (eds), The *gifted and talented: Developmental Perspectives* (pp 99-132), Washington, DC: American Psychological Association

White, J.P. (1972), 'Creativity and education: a philosophical analysis', in Dearden, R., Hirst, P., Peters, R.S., *Education Development and Reason*, London and Boston: Routledge & Kegan Paul

Woods, P. (1990), *Teacher Skills and Strategies*, Lewes: The Falmer Press

Woods, P. and Jeffrey, R. (1996), *Teachable Moments: The Art of Teaching in Primary School*, Buckingham: Open University Press

Zdenek, M. (1985), *The Right-Brain Experience*, London: Corgi Books

Chapter 2

A practical framework for creativity

Anna Craft

In this chapter I introduce a practical framework for exploring creativity, involving people, processes and domains.

Introduction

I want to begin by telling you about two children whom I know very well. Sabine and Jason live a couple of streets away from each other, a stone's throw from the Arsenal football stadium in North London. They go to the same state primary school and have been in the same cohort since they were five. Both are now eleven and about to move on to the secondary phase of their education.

When I first met Jason, he was 10. His reading age was at least three years below his chronological age, his grasp of maths was very basic and his concentration was very poor. He took little interest in learning at school, read only when made to and would happily spend most of his time in front of the TV or video. I suppose you could say that he was the embodiment of the under-achieving child which the media are so fond of describing.

Sabine on the other hand, when I first met her, had just completed her first novel. It was just 2,000 words long; but that is still quite an achievement for a nine year old. Her command of mathematics was strong and she was confident in dealing with abstract ideas. She was full of curiosity and always impatient to learn the next thing.

Sabine's parents are both professionals, Jason's run a small local business. Both their sets of parents are supportive and anxious that their child does well. Jason and Sabine are united in something else: both felt bored and disconnected with school, both were becoming difficult and causing problems for themselves and those around them.

They also face the same future, with its fragmenting communities, unstable markets and rapidly changing workplaces. For them there will be no certainties, no established precedent for the form of their working lives or guarantee of success in their chosen field. We know this already. It is already true for learner's leaving school *now* and probably *has been* for several years. But for Sabine and Jason, flexibility, ingenuity and an ability to learn quickly are going to be key for survival.

I believe that the education which Sabine and Jason were receiving was letting them both down in different ways. It seems to me that in their own ways both Sabine and Jason were struggling to reach their full potential in a school which did not engage with them creatively.

I am under no illusion about how difficult and demanding are the conditions under which their class teacher has to function. I acknowledge, along with other researchers (Woods and Jeffrey, 1996, Halliwell, 1993), that education is, fundamentally, creative. However, I believe that it needs to become much more so, both within *and* outside schools. Education policies such as the reforms brought about in England and Wales since the late 1980s, are what I would describe as *modernist* - ie aimed at a structurally fixed, bureaucratic, and relatively predictable, world. Their effect is to circumscribe the system in which teachers operate, and consequently to constrain imagination and leach the creativity from teachers themselves. In this chapter, I therefore address some of my critical comments at the current educational system. To help us get to grips with some of the practicalities, I will use a framework for analysing creativity in education.

Creativity as people, processes and domains

My suggested framework for thinking about creativity, involves *people, processes* and *domains*. Each offers a 'frame' or a perspective through which to observe and foster creativity. All are necessary parts of the whole.

A short-hand way of representing the framework which I am proposing looks like this; as you read through the chapter hopefully the diagram will begin to make sense!

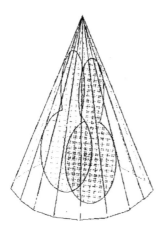

In other words, within (or indeed across) any domain, creativity involves aspects of the person, and also creative processes, some of which are part of the person. Of course, people are often creative in more than one domain.

My proposals have some ideas in common with those of Howard Gardner, already referred to in Chapter 1. However, there are some significant differences between us also. Before I explore my own framework in more detail, I will take a brief look at Gardner's ideas.

He has described (Gardner, 1983, 1993a) a framework for understanding creativity which involves 'intelligence, domain and field'. Originally formulated by Csikszentmihalyi (1988) and explored further by Feldman, Csikszentmihalyi and Gardner (1994), the idea is that creativity comes from the interactions of three 'nodes': the individual (and their intelligence), the domain and the wider field.

By 'intelligence' Gardner means inherited capabilities

of specific kinds. As he puts it: 'intellectual proclivities that are part of our birthright. These intelligences may be thought of in neurobiological terms' (1993a: page xx). His notion of 'multiple intelligences' was introduced in Chapter 1, where I indicated that his theories are under debate. One element of this debate concerns the role of genetic inheritance in the intelligences; his stance appears to be a controversial one.

By 'domain', Gardner means cultural arrangements of disciplines, crafts and other pursuits. Domains are therefore areas of human endeavour and understanding which can also be thought of in an 'impersonal' way as they all involve inter-related knowledge, understanding and skill. Intelligence and domain are not to be confused, Gardner argues, since any domain will require a range of intelligences. As he argues: 'the domain of musical performance requires intelligences beyond the musical (for example, bodily-kinaesthetic intelligence, personal intelligences) just as musical intelligence can be mobilized for domains beyond music in the strictest sense (as in dance or in advertising). (1993a: page xxi)

'Field' is a sociological description, which as Gardner puts it 'includes the people, institutions, award mechanisms, and so forth, that render judgments about the qualities of individual performances.' (1993a: page xxi)

Creative individuals, according to Gardner (and indeed others such as White, 1972), are those who consistently solve problems or create outcomes within a domain, and whose work is considered acceptable by members of a field. And this is where one of the main differences between my framework and Gardner's, lies.

For I would argue, along with others such as Cameron (1995) that all individuals are creative, in that creativity is a 'natural' part of life. As Cameron puts it: 'Creativity is the natural order of life. Life is energy: pure creative energy.' (1995: 3). Thus in my view, all individuals are creative. We all, at a fundamental level, have a capacity for innovation and development. This is part of the human condition - although of course it will vary in quality in extent. The recognition of the field toward that individual, and the individual's contribution to it, is thus not a key part of creative action in my framework. I am interested in what some people have called 'little c' creativity, rather than the 'big C' or 'high' creativity of the unambiguous cases of creative individuals drawn from the arts, sciences, humanities or spiritual arenas, where their achievements are acclaimed within their field and often beyond too.

Another difference between my framework and Gardner's is that I find his approach lacking holism, in two ways. First, his description of 'intelligences', although helpful in understanding different individuals' strengths, weaknesses and preferences, nevertheless seems to lack the notion of the 'person-as-a-whole'. In other words, it is a very intellectualist approach to capability. Consequently, my proposed framework incorporates Gardner's intelligences, within a wider grouping, 'people' - ie internal and external processes which are to do with human interaction with the environment.

Gardner's overall framework of intelligence, domain and field also seems to me to omit some core processes which would seem central in creating, whatever the domain or intelligences. Therefore I have introduced a third element, which examines some of the *processes* which creativity seems to me to involve. My framework draws on observations of educators at work with children as young as three, through to adults. I propose it as a possible way of thinking about creativity. As such, it is tentative.

People

Creativity is about people having mastery, or 'agency', over their environment. It is, in other words, about individuals being able to 'actualize' their choices in their lives, in a way which feeds their identity. As I said in Chapter 1, I find that humanistic psychology offers useful insights into creativity as self-actualisation. I want to emphasise six critical aspects of people and creativity: conscious and non-conscious 'self', choice, personal style, relationship, intelligence and essentialist characteristics.

Conscious and non-conscious self

To start then with the *conscious and the non-conscious self.* Here I draw on the psychosynthesis writer, Assagioli (1974), an Italian medical doctor and psychiatrist who practised and wrote in the early and mid-twentieth century. His theory is drawn from clinical observation over many years. He suggests we can think of ourselves as having two selves. Our conscious self, which is rationalist and aware, and the one we are not conscious of, which is more intuitive, impulsive, emotional and subject to sensation. Our conscious self, has *choice,* and can 'transcend' or rise above the deeper self, selecting out elements to emphasise.

This kind of idea of 'conscious' and 'unconscious' self is one which was developed by psychoanalytic theorists such as Jung and Freud, on whom Assagioli drew. It is also a distinction which some, especially those working on women's perspectives, such as Gilligan (1982, 1986, 1988) might challenge, in that the implication of the multiple self can be that the 'transcendent' self is super-ordinate and more important than the other selves. Nevertheless for me the model does describe an important separation between aspects of self, in which one has choice and the other does not.

Choice

The important idea of choice has also been developed by Fritz (1943). He contrasts behaving within a 'reactive-responsive orientation' to 'the orientation of the creative' (p43). Within the reactive-responsive orientation it is impossible for an individual to take charge of their own choices, or to exercise volition. The creative orientation on the other hand assumes that chosen results can occur - even if the actualising of them is not clear at the outset. Indeed, as Fritz puts it, 'in the creative orientation, what the creative person creates is something that never existed before' (p44). For Fritz, the prediction of the future by invention involves 'structural tension' which is the space between vision and current reality - overcome by concentrating on the vision, on the goal, or on the imagination. Both possibilities exist in all of us. Our transcendent self can, however, choose to focus on and emphasise creativity. So creativity is also about our transcendent self making choices.

So, Sabine's conscious self, chose to shape some of her dreams and other impulsive and play ideas, into a long story which became a 4,000 word story. And Jason's chose to invent recipes and menus, and to experiment with foods. Both chose what Fritz would call the creative orientation, in their area of creative expression. And in doing so, Sabine adapted existing characters in her stories to create a new plot, and Jason abandoned some of the conventional wisdom about food combinations, and innovated. He invented new recipes. You may by the way have recognised these children as those who participated in the 'passion assembly' in Chapter 1.

Personal style in creating

Here I want to highlight the distinction between adapting and innovating. Identified by Michael Kirton (1989), UK management theorist, who has worked for over twenty years on refining the theory, which is that there are two main styles of creative behaviour: adaptation and innovation. These are 'stable traits' within people. In other words, individuals tend to adopt one style or another, which remains stable across time and context. For Kirton, 'adaptation' is about accepting the existing framework around a problem, and finding a way of responding; it is about 'doing things better'. 'Innovating' on the other hand, is about being able to set aside accepted ways of doing things, and 'doing things differently' - even if there is a short term impact on efficiency. An innovator often consciously or unwittingly re-constructs the problem in trying to solve it. In schools, and in our education system more widely, we are very good at supporting adaptors and fostering adaptive behaviour. We are much less good at supporting innovators.

Relationship

Creativity inevitably involves 'being in relationship', or in dynamic interaction - with oneself, with other people, with the domain/s, or with all three. In my recent research project undertaken with Tom Lyons

(Craft, 1996a), several educators talked of being, as a teacher, in relationship with a subject they were teaching. In the same study, several others talked of empathising with learners.

It seems to me no co-incidence that learners and parents often refer to the quality of the relationship between the educator and the learner, and the educator and their subject, as a measure of perceived effectiveness in teaching. Both Sabine and Jason developed a relationship with their own chosen domain, but both had difficulty in making adequate relationships with their school teachers. Luckily, both developed stimulating relationships with educators outside of school (Sabine with her dad, and Jason with a local entrepreneur in the food business).

The importance of 'relationship' to learners is well-documented, both in terms of relationships between learners and in their relationships with educators (Cullingford, 1991, Delamont and Galton, 1987, Jackson, 1987, Pollard, 1987, Pollard et al 1997, Sluckin, 1987). Good educator-learner relationships are key to 'effective' teaching and learning (Cooper and McIntyre, 1996a, 1996b). And as any educator knows, key to fostering learning are positive and dynamic relationships where the teacher remains in control but the focus is on the learner. I call this approach 'teacher centred but learner focused' (Craft, 1996a and Craft et al, 1996b).

'Relationship' as a component of creativity, can also involve a need for audience. This can mean sharing the outcomes of creativity with other people, by talking about it, showing it, performing it, demonstrating it and so on. Some people feel a need to be witnessed by an audience. Sabine wanted her novel to be read by other people. Jason too, wanted others to try the fruits of his cooking. Audience was a theme arising for several educators in the research study which I mentioned above. What seems to link them all is a need to know from other people that what they have created has worth, whether it is an idea for arranging the classroom, an in-service session, or a new cake recipe (Craft, 1996a).

Sadly, for Jason and Sabine, their experience of school

learning was of their teacher planning for and teaching the class as a unit, rather than being able to build relationships with each of the children. I call this the 'teacher centred and *class* focused' approach (as opposed to teacher centred and *learner* focused). As a consequence of thinking of the children in achievement groupings and also as part of the whole class unit, Sabine's fascination and facility with words and creative writing, and Jason's passion for food and its preparation, were overlooked, until it came to the 'passion assembly' when each brought their passions from home in to the school environment.

Yet, many educators find the learners they work with a source of inspiration. These recent comments from primary teachers are not unusual: 'I think the kids keep me going to be honest... I enjoy it, I enjoy being with the kids, they give me a buzz' ... 'the children are the inspiration' (Craft, 1996a). So how can the real passions of some children get overlooked in school, in the way Sabine's and Jason's were? I think part of the answer lies in the creativity involving people having mastery; these two children found inadequate encouragement in school to develop mastery in the domains which they loved. Part of the *teacher's* mastery involves controlling the learning environment. There is a fine line between planning a structure for learning, and enabling children to come at this from their own perspectives. Particularly when, as in many schools, class sizes are large.

Intelligence

As described earlier, Gardner (1983, 1993a, 1996) has developed a theory of multiple intelligence. It is underpinned by what I will call a 'pluralist' view of mind. As he puts it, the theory recognises 'many different and discrete facets of cognition (1993a, p6), and acknowledges, rather like Michael Kirton, that 'people have different cognitive strengths and contrasting cognitive styles' (1993a, p6). Unlike Kirton's spectrum involving basically two styles, though, he proposes that there are an unknown number of basic and separate human capacities of which he has widely enumerated seven and more recently introduced other possibilities. He argues that the purpose of schools should be to develop intelligences appropriately for each individual. What Gardner suggests is that each individual learns better through some intelligences than through others. Clearly, applying Gardner's theory of multiple intelligences means accepting as a consequence that schools need to be geared more to the individual.

I want for a moment to consider the notion of non-conscious intelligence. A part of 'spiritual intelligence', by this I mean a connection with 'the universal energy' - or the energy of the universe, in a way which we cannot currently explain; I include in this forms of communication which are not verbal, synchronous 'happenings' and awareness which appears to transcend communication channels which we cannot understand easily. Parapsychologists such as Roney-Dougal (1994) devote their studies to trying to understand psychic phenomena such as telepathy (mind-to-mind communication), clairvoyance (obtaining information about, for example, lost objects which no-one knows about), pre-cognition (knowing about something that hasn't yet happened) and psychokinesis (affecting things outside of oneself just by thought alone). Roney-Dougal (1994) argues that spiritual awareness forges a link between science and 'magic' and that spirituality is an emerging form which will gradually ascend over other forms of intelligence. Indeed other writers (Redfield, 1994, Billen, 1996) have described the current era as an age of consciousness: spiritual intelligence can be thought of as being a part of this age.

By 'non-conscious intelligence' I mean the capacity to access Assagioli's 'Self' (1974) - the unconscious mind, the source of impulses, sensations and feelings, and which is often non-logical. There is an element of the non-conscious which some (eg Jung) have claimed to be somehow connected to other people - Jung called this the 'collective unconscious'. Some people seem particularly able to access their non-conscious, and the so-called collective unconscious (Edwards, 1993, Glouberman, 1989). I propose that accessing unconscious intelligence is a critical aspect of fostering creativity. I explore this further, with Tom Lyons, in chapter 7.

Essentialist personality and biographical factors

In Chapter 1, I noted some of the core qualities of the creating mind, drawn from various authors in humanistic psychology. Here I want to touch briefly on some personality and biographical factors which may be associated with 'high creativity' and possibly with creativity in general. I use the term 'essentialist' to mean 'essence'. I draw here on Gardner's (1993b) study of seven great creators (Freud, Einstein, Picasso, Stravinsky, Eliot, Graham and Gandhi), selected for their representation of the seven intelligences. There are, of course, problems with Gardner's selection: the study includes only one woman, it focuses on 'high creativity' only, it is time-bound and to an extent geographically/culturally bound (to Europe in the early 20th century). However, I believe that Gardner identifies a number of aspects of the behaviour of these creative people which provide interesting food for reflection in considering ordinary creativity.

Similarities between the seven creators, included 'rapid growth, once they had committed themselves to a domain' (p364). Another common feature was a level of self-absorption and self-promotion, in the interests of the work itself. Another similarity was 'the amalgamation of the childlike and the adultlike' (p365) (something emphasised by others, for example, the CBI Education Foundation in encouraging creativity and innovation in schools - 1994). Gardner noted that each experienced a feeling of being under siege during their 'greatest creative tension' (p367).

He also noted social-psychological similarities, for example that love, within the homes in which they each grew up, 'seems to have been conditioned on achievement' (p367), that each household was quite strict, so that 'ultimately, each of the creators rebelled against control' (p367), that each creator had a personal sense of social marginality, which they used 'as a leverage in work' (p368) to the extent that 'whenever they risked becoming members of 'the establishment' they would again shift course to attain at least intellectual marginality' (p368). He also described the ten year cycle of creativity experienced by each of these individuals, consisting of initial breakthrough followed by consolidation, succeeded ten years later

by a subsquent breakthrough which was more integrative, and so on and so on. He indicates that each of these creators was 'productive each day' (p372) - and that in the nature of their creativity, each demonstrated the capacity to identify and then explore 'asynchrony' with others within their field of endeavour. Breaking away from an established wisdom is in his view an essential aspect of the creative process as demonstrated by these seven individuals.

Some of the characteristics (childlike qualities, feeling under siege, being on the edge, high energy and productivity) which Gardner identifies, appeared among educators in the research project which Tom Lyons and I undertook from 1995-6 (Craft, 1996a). So, we might expect to see some of the qualities described above, in ordinary individuals: the childlike playfulness, the feeling of being under siege whilst being creative, the connection between love and achievement, the wish to be 'on the edge', high energy and productivity, and so on. And of course it could be that each kind of creativity involves different personal responses. For parents and teachers the feeling of being under siege for example is very common!

Processes

Creativity involves several interwoven processes, and it has a natural cycle. Over the years there have been many definitions of the processes involved in creativity. I want to focus on some drawn from recent research (Collings, 1989, Craft, 1996a, Craft et al, 1996b, Fryer and Collings, 1991, Fryer, 1996, Shagoury-Hubbard, 1996). These are summarised in the diagram below, which has as the source, 'impulse' - and which flows through to 'creativity as an approach to life'. Think of it almost like a geographic diagram of a slice through the earth, showing all the soil layers and sediments (Fig. 1)

Let me try and explain the diagram:

Impulse: feeds unconscious, intuitive, spiritual and emotional

The sources of creativity aren't always conscious or rational. At times we may not even be aware that

Fig. 1

CREATIVITY EVIDENT IN
APPROACH TO LIFE!

TAKING RISKS, AND THE CYCLE
OF CREATING

IMAGINATION: PROBLEM
FINDING/SOLVING, THINKING,

UNCONSCIOUS, INTUITIVE,
SPIRITUAL AND EMOTIONAL

IMPULSE (bedrock and source of
creativity)

the creative impulse involves thinking. The intuitive, spiritual and emotional also feed creativity, in ways which can be difficult to explain or describe. In Chapter 7, Tom Lyons and I explore this. For now, here is an example of how the intuitive seemed to inform a creative act. An educator participating in our recent research project woke up in the middle of the night with a new melody playing in her head. She hurried downstairs to the piano, and played it out. It eventually became the core theme to an end-of-term opera. (Craft, 1996a).

Sometimes, we are unable to articulate to ourselves what we know or can do - in which case we undergo experiences in a state of 'not-knowing- until a meaningful pattern emerges (Saltzberger-Wittenberg et al, 1983). When Jason is creating new recipes, he gets stuck for a few days and then suddenly it comes to him. His unconscious 'Self' is working on solutions to the problem, from which his conscious 'I' then selects an answer.

Imagination: problem finding/solving, and thinking

Creativity involves *using one's imagination* in any given situation: not being satisfied with what already exists, but considering other possibilities, which may include ones we do not yet know about. So, creativity also involves having original ideas, which can come from seeing connections between two or more seemingly unrelated things.

As the American researcher, Czikszentmihalyi, has said (1994), creativity is about both problem solving and problem finding. In other words, the formulation of a problem is just as important a part of creativity as the solving of one. I once asked Jason to think of a starter for my dinner party. I was inviting him to solve a problem, which Cziksentmihalyi calls this a 'presented' problem. He checked what kinds of food my guests might and might not eat, and also what the rest of the meal was to be. A week or so later, he invented a new idea using cracked wheat and chopped fruit.

On lots of other occasions, Jason found problems to solve, of his own accord. For example at the end of the last school year, his teacher left his school to move on to a new teaching post. His cohort of classmates decided to create a surprise party for her, and during playtimes, several children organised the making of a tape of her favourite music, and a short cabaret. Another child co-ordinated the making of cards for the teacher. It was Jason who realised that nobody had thought about refreshments, and called this to the attention of the whole group. Led by Jason, they worked out what they would like to have and how to get it. They reprographed a note to parents co-written by Jason and the head teacher requesting small food donations from parents. As a consequence a feast was collected. Thus Jason both 'found' and 'solved' the problem.

As touched on briefly in Chapter 1, creativity involves *divergent thinking* (what de Bono has called 'parallel thinking' (1995) - ie thinking from 'what if', association, intuition and possibility; beginning from questions - why? how else? Instead of thinking in a linear fashion). But creativity also involves *convergent thinking,* or finding possibilities which fit a set of needs; this is how the end-stage of problem solving is completed. The same creative act may involve both divergent and convergent thinking. When Jason recommended the starter for my dinner party, he used 'what if', or divergent thinking, finding combinations of foods which seemed initially un-related. But he also used convergent thinking: his idea had to fit in with the identifed needs.

Taking risks and the cycle of creativity

Being able and willing to have a go at expressing oneself is key, and thus it can involve *taking risks and being witnessed doing so.* Both Jason and Sabine took risks and were witnessed, in their different ways.

Creativity involves a cycle, which I think of as having five stages.

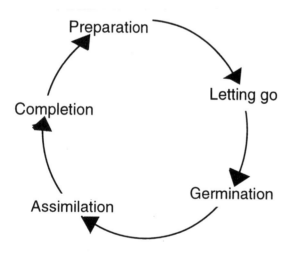

First, there is 'preparation' - getting in to an appropriate 'place' for being creative. This can mean a physical space, also an emotional space, it can mean making time, or being with other people who stimulate or support or both. Preparation can also mean reaching a point of frustration with an issue where one feels the need to make change happen. For Sabine, that was being at home, in a quiet corner of the kitchen, with her colouring pens and writing materials. She liked to know someone was around, usually her dad, who she could check out ideas with, and she also liked to draw the characters and situations in her stories. Sometimes she would feel terribly stuck and get quite bad tempered, before she could progress. I certainly know that feeling when I am writing!

Then, there is 'letting go'. In other words, a period of passivity, emptiness, lack of direction and loss, where the main activity is about letting go and surrendering control. For Sabine this was where her colouring pens would come in. Drawing the characters and situations was a way of letting her unconscious self give her ideas.

Letting go is followed by what Robert Fritz (1946) has called 'germination' (when the idea is conceived, often accompanied by a great burst of energy), during which 'excitement, interest and freshness abound... there can be great insight, realization, enthusiasm, change, and a sense of power' (p82). When Sabine was at this point she would chatter aloud, to her characters and to her dad, and would write furiously, and as fast as she could. It could be difficult to get her to stop for dinner!

The period of germination is followed by assimilation, like the gestation period of the human birth cycle. It is the least visible, and is an internal stage, which requires time to take root. For Sabine this would often take place on her walk to school, on the swings in the park, when playing with friends, at her drama group. She would gradually finalise ideas without really knowing how it happened.

The last stage, completion, involves the bringing to fruition of the idea which involves the capacity to 'receive' as well as to 'create' - in other word. Fritz likens it to giving birth. For Sabine this was when she put the story on to the computer and edited it to be just how she wanted it - although another child might consider the job completed before the story is edited.

A final aspect of the creative cycle is that *creativity*

increases and multiplies. Creativity leads to more creativity. Thus the cycle begins again, only this time there is more than one cycle generated by the previous one. Having invented one starter, Jason then went on to compile a whole series of them, getting permission to prepare them for his family during the half term week - a different one every other night. And he began to wonder about catering the starters for my dinner parties. He also began to wonder about going to catering school (which in fact he did, eventually, do). Sabine's first novel led on to another, with some of the same characters in it. She also made copies of the first one, and bound them. She circulated them to children who were interested in reading stories written by children, which led to the idea of starting a club, which she did. She also wrote a play based on the first novel, which the club performed to parents and interested others.

Of course, the process of creativity varies from person to person. Some people need a lot of time in the preparation stage, others get 'stuck' in the 'letting go' phase, others are very focused on the 'completion' stage and consequently have perhaps a more 'goals orientated' approach to their own creativity. The point is that there are many different paths to being creative, and that individuals have their own strengths and weaknesses in engaging with the process. And that there is no 'right way' of being creative.

So, from the creative impulse, through its forms of expression, I have suggested that creativity can be shaped, crafted and encouraged. What I am describing is *creativity evidenced in one's approach to life.* It may involve solving problems, but it is not exclusively about this. It is not exclusively about performance, or about thinking, or about painting, or about scientific method, or about algebra, or about dramatic play. It is about explicitly having one's approach to life in 'possibility mode' or 'what if' mode, in any domain.

Domains

The 'domain' provides the 'content area' in which a person operates their creative process, and I suggest it is a very important aspect of the framework for understanding creativity, because as I shall explore in Part 2 of the book, creativity is not 'content free'.

A domain can be understood in a variety of ways, but the way I am using it is to describe a body of organised knowledge, about a specific topic. By 'domain' I do not necessarily mean a subject area, for example 'the English language', as this is too big. But verbal communication, or 'speaking and listening' as it is described in the National Curriculum, would be a domain, as would 'literature appreciation'. They are distinct enough to be reasonably separate from one another, and yet to be recognised as both forming elements of the cluster of knowledge which we call 'the English language'.

Domains generally exist before a person contributes to or transforms them (although new domains have started throughout history; for example, social geography, electronic information exchange via computers and phone lines). Domains have a history which can be studied. Usually, domains are described through specially developed symbolic representation (for example words, music, algebraic algorithms, etc). The more that a person knows about a domain, the more they are able to evaluate the extent to which a new contribution to it is in fact creative (ie different). And it could be, as Gardner suggests (1984, 1993a, 1996) that our capacities in each of the different 'intelligences' dispose each of us toward one or another domain/s above others.

Obviously, creativity looks different in each domain, because each one involves different core concepts and behaviours. Thus creativity in arithmetic could mean finding more than one way of solving a numerical problem, demonstrated using deductive reasoning (ie 'if this happens then that will follow') and expressed in mathematical symbols. Creativity in social and personal interaction on the other hand could mean inventing a new game, or form of social gathering, using 'inductive reasoning' ('this kind of idea has worked in the past, so I'll expect it to again') and expressed in spoken or written words.

Creativity within each domain will change over time. For example, the invention of the skateboard was a creative development of roller skates. The ways in which children and adults use them developed very quickly through creative play in various parts of the world, to include fashionable acrobatics and dancing as well simply travelling fast!

Although creativity will look different in each domain, there are common features, such as the manifestation of some kind of transformation, through being open to lots of possibilities. Playfulness, and about being willing to have a go, are also features, as is *choosing* to express and apply our ideas.

My main reasons for suggesting domains are a part of the framework for thinking about creativity, is that the notion of domains gets us away from thinking that creativity is just about the arts. Creativity is about **all** knowledge. Considering the many domains of creativity also reminds us that the personal and process aspects of creativity are only a part of the picture, and not the whole of it.

Using the practical framework: an interpretive prism

There is an advertisement shown in British cinemas for some kind of alcoholic drink, in which a guest at a wedding looks at aspects of the celebration through the bottle of the spirit, which distorts the picture in amusing ways. I consider the practical framework for describing creativity as being rather similar, although hopefully less distorting! It is like a prism which enables us to split out three elements in each creative act: people, process, domain.

The prism is of course three dimensional, as the diagram on page 20 shows. Hopefully now it will make a little more sense.

When I shared this model with some educators recently at an *Education Now* conference on creativity, several colleagues suggested other metaphors for describing creativity - one being a crystal, which grows. I find this image compelling, as it has the potential to split, and represent, reality in many different facets.

Sabine's experience of personal and process aspects of creativity in the domain of creative writing were positive, although what her school contributed left a lot to be desired. Using the framework we can see she perhaps needed more stimulation in relationship with an educator in school, but was very confident in the process of creating, through which she was able to let her intuitive, unconscious self be expressed. The framework might also lead us to ask how far Sabine was experiencing creativity in other domains.

The framework enables us to see that Jason, too, perhaps lacked adequate relationships with educators in school. And that he was particularly good at taking risks, and using both divergent and convergent thinking. Again, we might ask how far Jason might be able to experience creativity in other domains.

As to the problem of how to provide stimulating relationships for each, some writers in this field (Fryer, 1996, Shagoury Hubbard, 1996, Torrance, 1984) advocate mentoring. All of these writers have recommended the key role of teachers and/or other adults as mentor (on a one-to-one basis) in supporting the development and expression of pupils' creativity. Shagoury Hubbard (1996) also talks about children taking on the mentor role where appropriate.

Mentoring enables someone with greater expertise to help someone with less expertise in any given domain. It is a similar idea to Vygotsky's notion of an expert 'scaffolding' the learning of a novice. Mentoring creativity means providing a role-model as well as direct support, for the learner. In other words, mentoring is one of the strategies which brings together the three aspects of creativity, the person, the process and the domain.

Summing up on the practical framework:

In this chapter I have introduced my framework for understanding creativity as involving people, processes and domains. I identified six core aspects of people:

* conscious and non-conscious self
* choice
* personal style
* relationship
* intelligence
* essentialist personal/biographical features

I have identified some of the creative processes, as follows, and introduced a model exploring ways in which they may interrelate together to produce a creative approach to life:

* impulse
* unconscious, intuitive, spiritual, emotional
* imagination
* taking risks and the cycle of creating

Finally I have introduced the notion of domains in which we create and foster creativity.

I have suggested that the framework should be used as a practical tool for fostering creativity in children. I have suggested that mentoring is one strategy which brings together the three elements of creativity. In Parts 2 and 3 of this book, I explore some of the learning implications of the framework, by looking at the practicalities of fostering creativity across the curriculum, and in cultural context. Part 4 addresses personal and system implications for educators, by looking at creativity and vision.

References

Assagioli, R. (1974) *The Act of Will*, London: Wildwood House

Billen, A. (1996), 'The New Age Gurus', *The Observer Life*, 1st September, 1996

de Bono, E. (1995), *Parallel Thinking: from Socratic to de Bono Thinking*, London: Penguin Books Ltd

Cameron, J. (1995), *The Artist's Way: A Spiritual Path to Higher Creativity*, London: Pan Books

CBI Education Foundation and The Department for Trade and Industry (1994), *Innovation: putting ideas to work*, London: UBI/Teacher Placement Service

Cooper, P and McIntyre, D (1996a), *Effective Teaching and Learning: Teachers' and Pupils Perspectives*, Buckingham: Open University Press

Cooper, P. and McIntyre, D. (1996b), 'The importance of power sharing in classroom learning', in Hughes, M (ed), *Teaching and Learning in Changing Times*, pp 88-108, Oxford: Blackwell

Craft, A. (1996a), 'Nourishing Educator Creativity: A Holistic Approach to CPD, *British Journal of Inservice Education*, Vol. 22, No. 3, Autumn 1996

Craft, A. with Shepherd, R., Pain, T. (1996b), *Creativity and Pedagogy in Spain: A study of twenty-seven teachers:* unpublished working paper, August 1996

Cullingford, C. (1991), *The Inner World of the School*, London: Cassell Educational Ltd

Csikszentmihalyi, M. (1988), 'Society, Culture and Person: A Systems View of Creativity', in R. J. Sternberg, ed *The Nature of Creativity*, New York: Cambridge University Press

Delamont, S., Galton, M. (1987), 'Anxieties and Anticipations - Pupils' Views of Transfer to Secondary School', in Pollard, A. (1987), *Children and Their Primary Schools*, London: Falmer Press

Edwards, G. (1993), *Stepping into the Magic*, London: Piatkus

Feldman, D.H., Czikszentmihalyi, M. and Gardner, H. (1994), *Changing the World, A Framework for the Study of Creativity*, Westport, Connecticut, London: Praeger Publishers

Fritz, R., (1943), *The Path of Least Resistance*, Salem, MA, Stillpoint

Fryer, M. (1996), *Creative Teaching and Learning*, London: Paul Chapman Publishing

Fryer, M., Collings, J.A. (1991), 'Teachers' views about creativity', *British Journal of Educational*

Psychology, 61, pp207-219

Gardner, H. (1984), *Frames of Mind: The Theory of Multiple Intelligences,* London: William Heinemann Ltd

Gardner, H. (1993a), *Multiple Intelligences: the theory in practice,* New York: HarperCollins Inc.

Gardner, H. (1993b), *Creating Minds: An Anatomy of Creativity Seen Through the Lives of Freud, Einstein, Picasso, Stravinsky, Eliot, Graham and Gandhi,* New York: HarperCollins Inc

Gardner, H. (1996), 'Are there additional intelligences? The Case for Naturalist, Spiritual, and Existential Intelligences', to appear in Kane, J. (ed), *Education, Information and Transformation,* Engelwood Cliffs, NJ: Prentice-Hall (forthcoming)

Gilligan, C. (1982), *In a Different Voice: Psychological Theory and Women's Development,* Cambridge, MA: Harvard University Press

Gilligan, C. (1986), 'Remapping development: the power of divergent data', in Crillo, L., Wapner, S. (eds) *Value Presupposition in Theories of Human Development,* Hillsdale, NJ: Lawrence Erlbaum Associates

Gilligan, C., Ward, J. V. and Taylor, C.V. (eds) (1988), *Mapping the Moral Domain,* Cambridge, MA: Harvard University Press

Glouberman, D. (1989), *Life Choices and Life Changes Through Imagework: The Art of Developing Personal Vision,* London: Unwin Hyman

Halliwell, S. 'Teacher creativity and teacher education', in Bridges, D. and Kerry, T. (eds) (1993) *Developing Teachers Professionally,* London and New York: Routledge

Handy, C. (1994), *The Empty Raincoat,* London: Hutchinson

Jackson, M. (1987), 'Making Sense of School', in Pollard, A. (ed), *Children and their primary schools,* London: Falmer Press

Kirton, M (ed), (1989, 2nd edition), *Adaptors and Innovators: Styles of Creativity and Problem Solving,* London: Routledge

Pollard, A. (1987), 'Goodies, Jokers and gangs', in Pollard, A. (1987), *Children and their primary schools,* London: Falmer Press

Pollard, A., Thiessen, D., Filer, A. (1997), *Children and their Curriculum,* London: Falmer Press

Redfield, J. (1994), *The Celestine Prophecy,* London: Bantam

Roney-Dougal, S. (1994), *Where Science and Magic Meet,* Shaftesbury, Element Books Ltd

Salzberger-Wittenberg, I., Henry, G., Osborne, E. (1983), *The Emotional Experience of Teaching and Learning,* London: Routledge and Kegan Paul

Shagoury Hubbard, R. (1996), *Workshop of the Possible: Nurturing Children's Creative Development,* Maine: Stenhouse Publishers

Sluckin, A. (1987), 'The Culture of the Primary School Playground, in Pollard, A. (ed), 1987), *Children and their primary schools,* London: Falmer

Torrance, E. P. (1984) *Mentor Relationships; How they Aid Creative Achievement, Endure, Change and Die,* Bearly, Buffalo, NY

White, J.P. (1972), 'Creativity and education: a philosophical analysis', in Dearden, R., Hirst, P., Peters, R.S., *Education Development and Reason,* London and Boston: Routledge & Kegan Paul

Woods, P. and Jeffrey, R. (1996), *Teachable Moments,* Buckingham: Open University Press

Part 2

Fostering creativity across the curriculum

Introduction

What does creativity look like in mathematics? In science? One of the myths which I meet often during conversations with teachers is the idea that creativity is just to do with the arts. In Part Two of the book, drawing on a range of case study data, I look at a number of subjects in the school curriculum, and explore both what creativity looks like and how it might be fostered in the classroom.

In these two chapters, I explore a variety of ways in which children's creativity might be fostered in the arts and humanities, also science, mathematics and technology. Chapter 3 explores the performing, expressive and visual arts, and also the humanities. In Chapter 4 the focus shifts to mathematics, science, information technology and design and technology. In both chapters I look at the kinds of purposes which might be served by fostering possibility thinking across the curriculum.

In a book of this length and scope it is perhaps inevitable that some areas are neglected. Thus, the early years curriculum is barely touched on in these chapters, and the nature of creativity in, for example, music, is omitted. But I hope, nevertheless that these two chapters will provide teachers with a range of ideas and possibilities for thinking about the nature and fostering of creativity in subjects other than the arts. If nothing else, I hope it will stimulate debate and experimentation.

Anna Craft

Chapter 3

I know where I stand with Arts and Humanities!

Anna Craft

The arts and humanities have an important place in fostering creativity in schools. In this chapter I look at how the arts have traditionally been seen as embodying and supporting creativity as reflections of and tools for analysing, aspects of life, starting by considering the sensory overlaps with science. I explore creativity in the performing, visual and expressive arts in school as enabling children to do, analyse and feel. Later in the chapter I look at ways in which learning in the humanities demands creativity of both children and teachers.

Real or imagined polarities?

The arts and humanities are often contrasted with science, maths and information technology as polar opposites. Indeed, as Taylor and Andrews (1993) point out, the coming of the National Curriculum has so altered the balance of science in the education of children 3 - 13, that the curriculum is 'led' by science in many schools. They claim that 'in many schools, a whole year's projects and topics are definitely listed in advance on staffroom notice boards, ensuring an inflexibility in learning - inert and sterile .... with cursory, superficial approaches to topic work, the arts frequently featuring as little more than servicing agencies for a science-driven curriculum.' (p131-2)

Embedded in some criticisms of the science-led curriculum is the belief that one of the differences between the arts/humanities and sciences is in the extent to which each subject involves or encourages creativity. I call this the 'polarity perspective' Contrary to this 'polarity perspective', I believe that each subject demands and fosters creativity. I explore in Chapter 4 how creativity is involved in the learning

and teaching of maths, science, IT and design and technology.

At the start of this chapter on the arts and humanities, I want to explore another dimension to the creativity of the sciences: the sensory aspect. Sensory experience is particularly relevant to science and, it has been argued (Best, 1990, Taylor and Andrews, 1993) that it forms a bridge, or even a place of overlap between the arts and science. I want to emphasis this sensory aspect and the different purposes it can play, in the arts and in the sciences. What is critical is that the differing purposes of sensory experience are drawn out with the children.

So, handling different kinds of materials may form part of a science activity; in constrast, observing them closely looking at line, texture, colour, imagining their history or future through play and fantasy, may form part of an arts activity. Watching the stick insects or looking after the class hamster may form part of the science curriculum in explaining behaviour, growth, habitat and camouflage, feeding and reproduction; handling, smelling, listening to and observing them may provide stimulus for creating, for example, poems, paintings, models, role-play, dance.

The way in which you set up sensory learning experiences then, depends on the purposes which you intend. I would argue, with Taylor and Andrews, that domination of the curriculum by science-led activities is not necessary, and that the polarity of creativity with the arts at one end and science at the other, is perceived and not real.

The creative arts and education for being

Part of the message of this book so far has been about embracing what David Fontana calls 'Education for Being' (1994, 1997). By this he means offering children 'the right to express their own feelings, to give their view of events, to explain themselves, to reflect upon their own behaviour, to have their fears and their hopes taken seriously, to ask questions, to seek explanations in the natural world, to love and be loved, to have their inner world of dreams and fantasies and imaginings taken seriously, and to make their own engagement with life.' (1997, p13). An education for being is about 'quality rather than quantity' (ibid p14) and it is about fully appreciating and becoming bound up in, the totality of the global environment, including the people in it. It is, as he puts it, 'an education that teaches children to understand and respect themselves, to empathize with others, to show a care and a concern for the world in which we live, to remain sensitive to the inner world of dreams, reflections and imaginings, to remain in awe of the wonders of creation, to give and receive love and understand the meaning of loving relationships, to express feelings and accept such expression in others, to identify worthwhile life goals and means towards their attainment, and to develop and articulate a mature philosophy of life that makes sense of the world and one's own place within it' (ibid, p14).

Maslow wrote in the 1980s about 'self-actualization' - in other words, adults who seem able to have become whole and complete people (1987). He noted that such people shared the following characteristics:

* being emotionally open
* spontaneity and 'being natural'
* being problem focused rather than self-focused
* being content with their own company
* having personal autonomy in attitude
* being accepting of self and others
* being appreciative of life
* capable of loving relationships
* being humorous
* being creative
* having an ethical framework
* operating to a democratic framework
* being consistent.

The notion is of a self-actualized person as a psychologically healthy one. David Fontana argues, and I would support his perspective, that an education for being supports children in their self-actualization.

As Fontana (ibid) and others (Gardner, 1994, Walters, et al 1996) note, the creative arts have a critical role to play, in fostering education for being, and as part of this, enabling individual learners to explore their own creativity and self-expression. Another way of describing these two roles of the arts is that they offer ways of *making* and ways of *appraising* (Robinson et al, 1990a, 1990b).

Theatre: playing with apples and dreams

In June, 1996, I organised a conference on Creativity in Education. Held in London, it was attended by educators from all over England, working in a variety of contexts, including youth work, primary and secondary school classrooms, universities and local education authorities, personal development and multi-media design. At it there were a number of speakers including Christine Kimberley, at that time one of the Directors of the Institute for Creativity. She spoke about the role of the Arts in fostering creativity. With her permission, I reproduce her talk here.

Making the Impossible Possible

Christine Kimberley, The Institute for Creativity

In the Spring of 1993 I was in Romania with a group of our students. We had been invited to attend the First International Meeting of European Drama Schools in Tirgu Mures, Transylvania. The festival was intended to offer an opportunity to both students and tutors to exchange skills, methods, philosophies and culture.

It was very successful and brought together groups from the former USSR, former Yugoslavia, Western Europe and Eastern Europe. For many groups, this was their first taste of performance and outside of their own cultural experience.

One morning, I was walking with Alina Cadariu, one of the festival organisers. A journalist and writer, she had an amazing English accent and command of the language.

She told me of a time some years ago when Ceaucescu came to visit his dasha in the hills just above Tirgu Mures. It was winter time and one of the town's officials decided it would be a wonderful idea to show Ceaucescu how productive the region was. So he imported crate upon crate of beautiful ripe apples and had them individually hung on all the winter bare trees in the orchards around the town.

Ceaucescu duly arrived, was very impressed, and expressed his wish that the whole of Romania be as fruitful and productive as Tirgu Mures.

We walked in silence for a while, lost in our respective thought. Then Alina turned to me and said that not so long ago, the possibility of walking and talking so openly and frankly with someone like me was only possible in her dreams.

When I started to think about this conference and what I might like to say, that conversation came to mind and I realised that when we come into this world we have two gifts. The physical resources of the planet we live on, including of course our own bodies and imagination. Two gifts, apples and dreams. No matter where we are born, irrespective of culture, race, religion, political context, economic circumstances. Two gifts. And these two gifts are essentially neutral. Innocent. Free from moral wrong. With them we create to live.

Imagination is the vehicle for change. First, we must imagine something is possible, then we can create a way of doing it.

Unfortunately, sometimes we have a tendency to invest the neutral facility, the innocent ability to imagine with the burden of outcome. It becomes tangled with the responsibility for moral wrong - and often with guilt, failure and even punishment.

It is then that we keep our imaginings to ourselves and feel powerless in the face of change - in the face of other people's imaginings.

There is a place where our imagination can run free. Where we can experiment and explore. Explore the 'what if' - safely free from the burden of outcome. This place for me is live Theatre. I believe it is true of the other arts too, but Theatre is my speciality.

In Theatre, Imagination is practiced, honoured, respected, experienced and witnessed, in innocence. For this very fact alone, Theatre is not a luxury or a pastime. It is an essential part of any robust, healthy society.

Theatre, like all the Arts, constantly reminds us that we have imagination. That imagination has infinite power to create possibility, diversity, solutions. In Theatre, we can explore death without dying. And without shedding a single drop of blood, we can reflect, judge, consider, discern and contemplate the most colossal or the most intimate of human dilemmas - in innocence.

I believe this is vital to us all. Particularly for young people, to have access to art and theatre - not just as doers, in taught classes, but as watchers, as audience.

In this capacity they have the chance to explore and to develop their own morals, ethics and so on through the act of witnessing. And, they are exposed to the impossible being made possible - as they are taken on an emotional, sensate journey - shown a story that they know to be both real and unreal all at once. Imagination in practice as they practice using their own. And this is the point, Theatre can't but encourage young people to wonder, to question, to use their imaginations, to explore possibilities. This is true learning as they learn to create their future.

It's no wonder that in countries with oppresive regimes of any persuasion, Art is held under strict government control. Artists are prosecuted. In such circumstances Art is dangerous. It might just awaken the artist - the imaginer - in everyone. They might just imagine and create the world they really want.

I'm sure that is why so much of Eastern Europe's theatre is so rich, so vivid, so vibrant, so metaphysical. It's been keeping the dreams of a culture alive - by keeping the imaginations alive. By constantly making the impossible possible -

keeping possibility for change alive.

The Institute for Creativity is an arts based organisation. We work with people's imaginations, their belief systems. Belief systems that sometimes hold people back from what they know they desire. Fulfilling what they feel and know deep inside. We will create in our minds, in our feeling selves, and if we can only allow these imaginings to be witnessed in innocence then perhaps we can create a truly non-abusive society.

(Kimberley 1996)

Of course, the role of theatre in particular and also the wider arts more generally, within a society, is culturally and era-specific. What they provide within any one society can be described along a continuum with at one end 'challenging society' and in the middle of it 'reflecting society' (at the far end might be 'supporting society', or hegemony). Focusing on the challenging and reflecting roles, Robinson et al (1990b) write, 'in some societies and at some times the artist is an iconoclast who challenges prevailing attitudes and values, generating new perceptions to challenge established ways of thinking. At others, artists are the 'voice of the community', shaping images and artefacts to give form to a community's deepest values and convictions' (p 29).

Christine emphasised the role of theatre in allowing us to explore all kinds of possibilities. She talked of our having two resources: the physical environment of our planet, and our imaginations.

Consider how often you utilise drama and theatre to help children draw on these two resources, and to ask 'what if?'

The performing arts: child as communicator, interpreter, creator

Drama, music, dance, physical agility, poetry reading and storytelling are some of the most common forms of performance in schools. Each gives children opportunities to communicate, to interpret, and to create for themselves. Tambling (1990) has argued, 'the arts are primarily about creativity and imagination'

(p95). It is important that we don't forget to encourage children to create for themselves, whether through story, rhythm, melody or choreography. Consider Morwenna.

Morwenna teaches Y5 children in a Northern city, in a school which is committed to teaching the whole curriculum through an arts focus. She herself is musical, and performs in local pubs as a folk singer playing her guitar, on a regular basis. She encourages the children to create their own drama, music, stories and dance as much as possible. At the end of each half-term of learning, she asks the children to work collaborative in small groups to create a performance piece which for them summarises what they feel they have learned. After a recent project on local history, one group of five children composed a song accompanied by xylophone, drum, triangle and recorder, which outlined all that they had both enjoyed and learned in the project.

How often do the children you teach have such opportunities to interpret, create and communicate?

Where children are performing a piece created by someone else, there is an important dynamic between 'author' (the choreographer, writer, composer) and the performers - even where the children don't get the chance to meet the author. "Being in relationship" is an important aspect of creativity. You can offer children ways of exploring what they consider the author's intentions to have been, and encourage exploration of possibilities in representing the work. Predicting how the author might then perceive the children's interpretations is a further aspect of fostering the children's creativity. Occasionally, it might even be possible to check out the author's intentions and reactions, face to face.

Creativity, or possibility approaches, can be fostered both *in* and *through* the arts: a notion explored by Robinson et al (1990 b), and which I will return to later when exploring the humanities.

Language and literacy

Language is a medium through which possibility can be explored. Like the performing arts, the creator (speaker or writer) can represent, analyse and express feelings. But what is different in the case of language is that particularly in the 3-13 age range, 'teaching the basics' is part of the focus. It has been argued (Taylor and Andrews, 1993) that the National Curriculum's definition of the language curriculum for schools has virtually divorced the learning of basic skills from the creative possibilities offered by language. In contrast I would argue that even with very young children it is possible to encourage experimentation, analysis and the expression of feelings.

Consider story time in the nursery: sharing books together offers opportunities for analysis - for example, exploring:

* the author's intentions,
* characterisation,
* plot,
* presentation,
* illustration.

It also an opportunity for exploring how the children feel about the story, as well as feelings within it. And there are plenty of ways in which story time can stimulate the children's own invention:

* predicting the ending, or thinking of alternative ones once you know how the story goes,
* making up rhymes and raps,
* inventing new characters,
* getting in to character and exploring the relationships between characters in the story through drama....

Similarly, teaching writing skills in the reception class can offer many opportunities for children to create, alongside developing the basics. Handwriting practice can provide the basis for imaginative work: for example by using poems and rhymes introduced and created verbally with the children during story times. The children's own writing at this age is often linked with their drawings: drawing their 'news' or 'writing about a picture' are common approaches. Although both involve the children making something, neither of these however is particularly creative. Other, more creative, possibilities include:

* responding to first hand experiences (such as a walk in the park, a visit to a puppet theatre, holding the class hamster, watching the tadpoles grow),

* inventing characters (creatures or people), objects and events   around which to design a story (this can be done individually, in pairs, groups or even as a whole class activity),

* conjecturing/exploring how something 'works' (such as the rising   of dough, the growing of cress, or collage work done by a partner),

* making signs for class-wide dramatic play (for example, turning the home corner into a hospital, a vet's or a shop),

* inventing five-word poems which embody their feelings about a particular event (such as bonfire night, a religious festival, an assembly by an older group of children or by themselves, a book which they have read or had read to them, the birth of a sibling, the death of a pet).

And of course writing creatively may be linked to other activities which themselves have potential for developing creativity, such as role play or reading. As the National Curriculum Council Oracy Project argued during the 1980s, oral language forms a vital part in fostering inspired written work in the classroom. With young children this is particularly so, as Cowie (1989) has documented; three year olds are capable of composing stories using emergent writing and drawing, and can tell these aloud. We know from work by Scarlett and Wolf (1979) who explored ways in which children's imaginative writing was enhanced by props (eg a dragon, a castle, a royal family, little trees and toy animals), that four year olds and upward are much more able to express their stories linguistically. The younger children needed much greater physical contact with their props in order to invent. From my own observations of under-4s, I would argue that encouraging and engaging in imaginative play with the children is vital to creativity. It can provide models of creating processes, and can stimulate the children's writing, particularly storying (ie the development of stories, through a variety of means, often collaborative, and given a variety of forms of expression).

Opportunities for developing creativity then, even at the most basic levels of language and literacy, do exist. As the child's skill progresses, the opportunities extend, as their more skilful use of language enables them to both explore other people's compositions and create those of their own. I was recently given a poem written by a ten year old boy whom I know. His name is Jack, and he wrote the poem in school, after he had had two teeth extracted. With his permission, I reproduce his poem here.

Oh Good Grief, Lost Two Teeth
By
Jack Penny

I went for an X-Ray on Friday.
It was not much fun at all.
I said, 'I'm not going. No way!'
Mum said, 'Well you'll have to babysit Paul!'
'Oh OK', I said. 'But it had better not hurt.'

'Sit down on the chair' said Mum.
I sat down. It was uncomfortable.
The nurse had a rather large bum.
The bright light was so horrible.
The nurse had a partner called Bert.

The X-Ray was sent to my dentist
And we had to wait a few weeks.
I hoped the dentist was not an apprentice
When it came to pulling out teeth.
What if he's even a nerd!

He showed me all his instruments.
In fact he was really quite nice.
I hope I don't have any more appointments
I really don't want to go twice.
I'll tell you what next occurred.

He pulled out his injector!!
To make my two teeth dead.
My mum was like a protector.
I immediately turned very red.
My eyesight even went blurred!!

He pushed and pulled on my teeth
And it hurt as he pulled them out.
I could hear the cracking. 'Oh good grief!'
I tried very hard not to shout.
Having two teeth extracted, I wouldn't like a third.'

What leaps out of Jack's poem for me is his capability in expressing what Wilkinson et al (1980) term 'affect' (ie 'emotional, imaginative and interpersonal awareness). Evidence from their Crediton Project which explored the writing of one hundred and fifty children aged 7,11 and 13, suggested that the younger children in the sample were less capable of expressing 'affect' than the older children.

However, other work (Graves, 1983) suggests that given the opportunities to draft, to discuss sources, to explore meaning and depth in their writing, young children are able to create complex and imaginative pieces. A number of researchers (Graves, 1983, Cowie and Hanrott 1984) argue that the following strategies help younger children's linguistic expression, including their writing. They are all aspects of developing what Graves named the 'writing community', and what I call a community of creators:

* allowing children control over their writing processes, which can mean giving the children time to compose,

* encouraging collaborative work some of the time,

* emphasising a range of audiences for writing (such as for each other, for younger children, for oneself, for parents, for the local community, as well as for the teacher),

* encouraging children to use the word-processor for drafting, editing and re-drafting,

* listening carefully to the children's views of and

reactions to writing,

* entering into the imaginative worlds which children create in their stories.

The arts and children's feelings

So far I have talked mainly about the expressive, performing (and to a limited extent, the visual) arts as both

* enabling children to do, or to make, and also

* enabling them to perceive, or analyse or explore, what they are representing.

But there is a third, important function of the arts, which is highlighted by Taylor and Andrews (1993) and also by Gardner (1994), and which should have become apparent in the poem above:

* enabling children's feelings.

One theory of rationality and feeling, put forward by Best (1992), is that children need to be introduced to the conventions and values of any particular art form in order to fully experience the 'relevant' feelings. Best's arguments are of course open to the charge of elitism and exclusivity. However there are two points embedded in his perspective, which I would argue are valuable in the primary classroom. First, that the domains of existing knowledge and achievement are an important and, I would argue, necessary backdrop, to exploring a 'feelings response' to art created by the children themselves and by others. Second, that children's feelings responses are probably deepened and broadened by an understanding of artistic genre and context. Meet, for example, Clare, developing the visual arts.

Clare teaches Y5 children in a city primary school. She has decided to devote a half term of art lessons exploring expressionist painting techniques and the context to the expressionist movement. The children learned about some of the key expressionist painters and their lives, by visiting several art galleries in London. Clare borrowed a selection of resources,

including a number of reproduction paintings by expressionists, from the resource bank of her LEA. The children's own art work included trying out various paint techniques, also painting replicas of particular reproductions in order to try these out.

The children's capability in exploring mood, movement, activity, relationships and so on, as represented in famous artists' work was gradually enhanced over the six weeks of this unit of work.

I would argue that this tiny snapshot of Clare's practice represents the importance and the potential, of exploring the domain to which any form of expression belongs, and the culture surrounding that domain. It also illustrates the primary and secondary sources which formed part of the children's learning. Their own creativity was encouraged within a defined context. Although this example is taken from visual art, the expression of feelings is also a part of the expressive and performance arts.

Consider your own practice in, for example, PE, drama or writing. How could you develop your own strategies for immersing children in existing knowledge and achievement, whilst also giving them an opportunity to explore their feelings?

Risk and ownership

One of the biggest challenges for children when creating in the arts is having a go at making something which they 'own'. This can carry considerable risk for children, as they may create something which does not meet with the approval of the intended audience. Although as Hargreaves, Galton and Robinson (1989) note, primary teachers in particular often try to support children's creativity in the arts in a two-stage process (ie modelling, or giving a lot of guidance to begin with), the evidence suggests that this does not in fact foster children's creativity (Galton, 1987). Instead, it seems (Armstrong, 1980, Rowlands, 1984) that what is really critical is that children understand the purposes of each activity, and the expectations of the teacher of what they are going to be doing. There is also a need to allow children time to incubate their ideas, and to come to terms with the challenges of risking failure, before owning their creative work.

Summing up on the arts

I have explored ways in which the arts enable:

* the development of children's imaginations in making or doing,

* children's skills in analysing and interpreting,

* exploration and expression of the children's feelings.

I have explored the roles played by the arts in both reflecting and challenging society, at different times in different cultures. The arts enable communication. I have argued that introducing children to existing domains of artistic expression is an important part of developing their own creativity and appreciation of the creativity of others. I have suggested that fostering creativity in the arts can involve risk for the children and consequently needs incubation time.

Learning about, for and through the humanities

Back in the 1970s, Alan Blyth and colleagues coined a way of thinking of the humanities as playing three roles in the 8 - 13 school curriculum, in that it was possible to educate *about, for and through* them (Blyth et al, 1978).

These models are, to my mind, still valid today, at the end of the 1990s and are, I would suggest, just as relevant for much younger children. They can be seen as three different and co-existent models of the curriculum. Learning *about* the humanities can be interpreted as a model of the curriculum as cultural transmission. Learning *for* the humanities implies a use of the knowledge and skills which will follow from the learning, and hence implies an instrumental, or utilitarian view of curriculum. Learning *through* the humanities implies a developmental view of the curriculum where the personal 'sense-making' learning of individual children is more deeply

emphasised than the transmission of a body of knowledge or the use to which this may be put later (Ahier and Ross, 1995).

Of course, the National Curriculum does provide a framework for both learning *about* and to a lesser extent, learning *for*. But it is much more down to you as the teacher to look at how to set up learning *through* for example history and geography.

The humanities: imagining different possibilities

Just as theatre enables us to explore imaginative possibilities in life, so history and geography can provide ways in to understanding multiple perspectives on aspects of life. I would argue that the humanities in particular offer children a model of imagination and creativity, because they are, in large part, about understanding human experience and behaviour.

Inevitably learning history and geography will take children beyond their own personal experiences, into other people's perspectives. These will often involve controversy and debate. For example:

* Interviewing a grandparent about their childhood;

* Hearing about different people's views about a proposed local road by-pass;

* Learning about the roles of different people in the school community - and their perspective on the school itself;

* Talking to someone who is or who has been, on strike;

* Conducting a survey among parents about their shopping habits to explore reliance on local stores versus large supermarkets;

* Participating in a debate about whether we should eat meat;

* Discussing the pros and cons of advertising (needs versus wants).

It seems to me that the humanities both require and foster the approach to life which starts with 'what if?' They demand of learners that they apply imagination to their existing and received representations of life.

I would argue that whichever model or combination of the three models you adopt in teaching the humanities in your own practice, *each* demands the development of imagination and creativity in children. The humanities are not value-free, as I shall explore in a brief look at history and geography.

Values in history and geography

History is an interpretive field: it is about interpreting evidence to piece together events and perspectives of people who, more often than not, lived before our own lifetimes. Historians themselves are working with 'leftovers' from earlier times, and need to exercise both keen observation and analysis, with imagination, to try and understand what different pieces of evidence might be saying about life in an earlier period. Teaching children this central idea involves both imagination and creativity. Working on actual primary sources may not be possible particularly with younger children, but the idea of working with incomplete left-overs can be simulated in the classroom and locality using accessible resources, such as pictures, artefacts, simple written sources, buildings, oral accounts. Theatre, simulation and dramatic play can help children take on the perspectives of people living in different eras, and of different people living in the same era.

It has been argued that history has traditionally been about, and documented by, men, and the history curriculum in schools is almost exclusively a white, male story. So, developing creativity in history also means encouraging children to ask questions about this and other assumptions which underly some of the received knowledge which they will meet.

Similarly, until about twenty years ago, the study of geography in schools was far more about the physical side of the subject (mapping skills, geology, patterns in the environment) than about the social. But as the field itself has evolved, so has the school curriculum so that even with very small children it now incorporates the study of peoples and their impacts on each other and their environments. I would argue, with Edwards and Knight (1994) that

In a democracy committed to human rights, liberty and equality, intolerance of others is a cause for considerable concern, especially as Britain develops an identity as part of Europe rather than as the leader of many countries... geography is important as a human subject in a humanistic society.

(Edwards and Knight, 1994, p68)

Although they are referring to the early years primarily, this notion of geography as being a moral study certainly holds with the older years. One of the main concerns of geography has to be about understanding the different perspectives of people living in different places, or belonging to different interest groups in the same place. And it will involve coming to have a sense of what it *feels* like to take on those different perspectives. Feeling, as Mary Warnock (1976) has argued, is absolutely central to imagination.

Summing up on the arts and humanities:

I have suggested that the humanities involve imagining different possibilities, offering:

* multiple perspectives on the present and the past (both descriptive and analytical),
* exploration of values and assumptions embedded in 'received' knowledge.
* opportunities for investigating human impact on the environment (other people as well as the wider world) - ie exploration of the morality of human action).

The arts and humanities offer many ways of developing creativity. They can provide bridges with the sciences through sensory experience, visual experimentation and critical analysis. In this chapter I have tried to demonstrate some of the ways in which the arts and humanities play a key role in the curriculum for children aged 3 - 13, in supporting the development of children's creativity.

References

Ahier, J., Ross, A. (1995), Introduction, in Ahier, J., Ross, A. (eds) (1995), *The Social Subjects within the Curriculum,* London: Falmer

Armstrong, M. (1980), *Closely Observed Children: Diary of a Primary Classroom,* London: Writers and Readers

Best, D. (1990), *Arts in Schools: A Critical Time,* Birmingham Institute of Art and Design, an NSEAD Occasional Publication

Best, D. (1992), *The Rationality of Feeling,* London: Falmer Press

Blyth, W.A.L. (1976), *Place, Time and Society 8 - 13: Curriculum Planning in History, Geography and Social Science,* Bristol; Collins/ESL

Cowie, H. (1989), 'Children as writers', in Hargreaves, D.J. (1989), *Children and the Arts,* Buckingham: Open University Press

Cowie, H. and Hanrott, H. (1984), 'The writing community: a case study of one junior school class', in H. Cowie (ed), *The Development of Children's Imaginative Writing,* London: Croom Helm

Edwards, A., Knight, P. (1994), *Effective Early Years Education: Teaching Young Children,* Buckingham: Open University Press

Fontana, D. (1994), *Growing Together: Parent-Child Relationships as a Path to Wholeness and Happiness,* Shaftesbury: Element Books

Fontana, D. (1997), 'Childhood and an Education for Being', *Caduceus Issue 34, Winter 1996/7,* Leamington Spa, Caduceus Publications Ltd

Galton, M. (1987), 'An ORACLE chronicle: a decade of classroom research', *Teaching and Teacher Education,* 3: 299-313

Gardner, H. (1994), *The Arts and Human Development,* New York: BasicBooks

Graves, D. (1983), *Writing: Teachers and Children at Work,* Exeter, NH: Heinemann

Hargreaves, D.H., Galton, M.J., and Robinson, S. (1989), 'Developmental Psychology and Arts Education', in Hargreaves, D.J. (1989), *Children and the Arts,* Buckingham: Open University Press

Kimberley, C. (1996), 'Making the Impossible Possible', in Craft, A. (ed), (1996), *Conference Proceedings: Creativity in Education Conference,* held in London, June 1996, Milton Keynes: The Open University

Maslow, A. H. (1987), *Motivation and Personality,* New York and Cambridge: Harper & Row, 1987

Robinson, K., Wills, G., Allen, D., Henderson, J., Everitt, P. (1990a), *National Curriculum Council Arts in Schools Project: Practice and Innovation,* Harlow: Oliver & Boyd

Robinson, K., Wills, G., Allen, D., Henderson, J., Everitt, P. (1990b), *National Curriculum Council Arts in Schools Project: A Curriculum Framework,* Harlow: Oliver & Boyd

Rowlands, S. (1984), *The Enquiring Classroom,* London: Falmer Press

Scarlett, G. and Wolf, D. (1979), 'When it's only make-believe; the construction of a boundary between fantasy and reality in story-telling', in Gardner, H. and Winner, E. (eds) (1979), *Facts, Fiction and Fantasy in Childhood,* San Francisco, Jossey-Bass

Tambling, P. (1990), *Performing Arts in the Primary School,* Oxford: Blackwell

Taylor R., Andrews, G. (1993) *The Arts in the Primary School,* London: The Falmer Press

Walters, J., Plasket, J., Andrews, B., Powell, K., Moskowitz, J. (1996), *Research on the Programs of the Aesthetic Education Institutes; The Final Report to the Lincoln Center Institute,* Harvard University, Cambridge: Project Zero

Warnock, M (1976), *Imagination,* London: Faber and Faber

Wilkinson, A., Barnsley, G., Hannah, P. and Swan, M. (1980), *Assessing Language Development,* Oxford: Oxford University Press

Chapter 4:

But some subjects just aren't creative....

Anna Craft

Or are they? In this chapter I focus on some school subjects which sometimes get ignored in discussions of creativity. I explore how creativity is fundamental to maths and science. I also look at design and technology, including information technology. How can a computer offer scope for creativity? How do you foster design and technology as an authentic activity for children in practice? Finally I look at the social implications of doing so.

Thinking mathematically

Mathematics is a way of thinking. It has a language system of its own, made up of figures and symbols. It is essentially about representing relationships in the world, and manipulating them. Whether we are talking about number, algebra, shape and space, data handling, etc., each mathematical topic contains a range of basic concepts which, once grasped, can give even very young children access to all kinds of exploration.

Knowing the basics

Just as we need words, spoken and written, as a tool to help us express our thinking in linguistic parts of the curriculum, at any level of mathematics children need to have learned some of the basic concepts in order to be able to explore with them. But even with a very early grasp of a mathematical concept it is possible to begin thinking mathematically, as these two examples show.

Ola, aged five, was sorting plastic cars and other shapes into sorting hoops. He had been asked to sort 'all the cars and all the green things', and he set out two hoops initially, until he came to a green car which belonged in both hoops. After a long think, he overlapped the sorting hoops and continued. The following day he chose to work in the maths corner during 'choosing' time, and explored sorting with duplo, using a number of different categories, such as 'all the squares and all the blue things', 'all the people and all the cars' and so on. In each case he found that there was at least one piece which belonged in more than one category. By the end of the day he had discovered that he could use a number of sorting hoops at once, and that they could overlap with one another.

Eloisa and Wale, aged 8, were working on some missing number questions which involved creative arithmetic. They each had a list of number statements which were incomplete, and which used all four number rules, for example

$15 = \underline{\quad} + \underline{\quad}$

$15 = \underline{\quad} - \underline{\quad}$

$15 = \underline{\quad} \times \underline{\quad}$

$15 = \underline{\quad} \text{ divided by } \underline{\quad}$

$15 = \underline{\quad} + \underline{\quad} - \underline{\quad}$

$15 = \underline{\quad} \underline{\quad} \underline{\quad}$

Having each found a list of possible solutions, they compared notes with one another.

Confidence and conjecture

We know that confidence in our own mathematical thinking can make a big difference to the ways in which we enable children to engage with the subject. Briggs (1989) has explored primary teachers' attitudes to mathematics. Her investigations illustrate that our own experiences of learning mathematics often contribute more to the way we feel about the subject, than the actual content. Some of the experiences which she describes as contributing to lack of confidence in the subject are:

* memories of failing.

* an emphasis on speed of working, with the associated (and false) expectation that mathematicians find answers to problems almost instantly

* for women in particular, the view that maths is a male domain, and a perception of their own teachers' expectations that boys will find it easy while in contrast girls are less likely to achieve success.

A learning environment which is one of either knowing or not knowing, succeeding or failing, can result in some of these feelings. It can lead to learners feeling exposed and threatened. On the other hand, a learning atmosphere which values conjecture and possibility, is one which enables everyone to try out their mathematical thinking.

Possibility language and mathematics

An aspect of creating a conjecturing atmosphere is to encourage children to couch their ideas in terms like 'perhaps if' or 'I suggest that', or 'maybe if'... In an environment like this, it is the responsibility not only of the teacher, but of the children as well, to be aware of the differing levels of confidence and knowledge, and to work together to allow everyone to express their ideas at the level that they are able to. You may be able to recall occasions when you have felt a sense of relief when someone else has voiced a question which had been puzzling you also, but which you perhaps felt nervous of asking. A conjecturing atmosphere, where the language of possibility is valued, encourages children to speak up when they are not certain.

Whether you teach maths as a whole class activity, in small groups or individually, children will engage much more creatively with any maths topic if possibility language is the way in which they communicate their thinking.

The maths scheme and maths activities

Most primary teachers use a maths scheme as the backbone of their work in this subject. And they do have lots of advantages:

* it is often possible for children to work at different paces from one another;

* they can be useful for helping children practise techniques (such as the number algorithms, or finding the area of a shape) or knowledge (such as number bonds or times tables);

* many maths schemes contain mathematical investigations.

As in any subject however, the text book is only a part of your resources. Setting up activities for the children to investigate either individually or collaboratively which involve applying the basic concepts which they have learned is really essential to enable their mathematical thinking.

Activities which enable mathematical creativity

Activities which generate more than one conjecture provide opportunities for creativity. Enabling children to engage with maths creatively means encouraging them to use maths as a tool, both for its own sake and for some practical purpose, having negotiated some shared understandings as a starting point, as this example may illustrate:

Ben was helping his class of 6 and 7 year old children come to recognise features of 3-D shapes. He began by negotiating some shared understandings by using a 'feely bag', along with one of each of the solid shapes in it. The children took it in turns to have a go at recognising through touch, then naming a shape, and finally withdrew it from the feely bag to compare with the shapes on display. Doing this meant he could get children thinking about the relevant criteria - which were to do with shape. Using the feely bag was a gentle strategy to help the children learn that some criteria, such as colour and texture, are not relevant in naming a 3-D shape. Having done this activity a few times, Ben encouraged the children to build and therefore experiment with the properties of 3-D shapes by providing lots of shape blocks in the construction area. Later he showed the children how artists and architects have used shape. He set each child a one-day mini project on 3-D shape, identifying a question to find out answers to. The children's projects included 'What is the best way of storing the big and little PE balls?', 'Why are there different patterns of brick in our school wall?' and 'Why don't builders use spheres?' Finding answers to their questions involved a mixture of convergent and divergent thinking.

As the example indicates, activities which enable creativity in maths can also need time and simple practical resources. Most people, adults and children, need concrete evidence for their mathematical thinking, and enough time to first see, then explore, patterns. Representing mathematical thinking through pictures (diagrams, number lines, sets etc) and symbols, is another way of seeing concrete evidence, as Haylock and Cockburn (1989) demonstrate in their work on early years maths. They argue that it is only having represented their mathematical thinking in some way, that children can generalise their ideas about any aspect of maths.

Summing up on maths and creativity:

I have suggested that children can be encouraged to use possibility language in order to conjecture in mathematics, within the parameters of their conceptual knowledge. A knowledge of the basics (concepts and language), and fostering confidence in oneself as a teacher, are important if you are to enable children to apply possibility thinking.

I have suggested that activities which enable multiple conjectures encourage children's creativity in mathematics, and that maths schemes whilst useful for building the basics, should form only a part of the repertoire of resources for supporting the mathematical thinking of children aged 3 - 13. There are of course exceptions; some schemes encourage children to make multiple conjectures.

Science and creativity

Some of the most creative people the world has seen have been mathematicicans or scientists, or both. Think of Einstein, drawn here by Francesca (aged 8) - or before him, Newton. Or Marie Curie. Or....

Representations of science

As Patricia Murphy's work (1994) illustrates, when children are asked to draw a picture of a scientist they often draw someone (usually a man) in a white coat, experimenting with strange liquids and long mathematical formulae, in order to invent something, illustrated by the pictures below drawn by children in Y5. I had asked the children to draw me a scientist (Fig. 2). The notion of the scientist as an inventor seems to be embedded in the ways children (and also many adults) think of science. This is as true of science in the classroom as it is beyond.

Fig. 2
Pictures drawn by Louis (9), Jack (10), Ashford (9),
Holly (10), Belle (10), Stephanie (10)

Children as scientists

A huge part of science is the process of investigation. This is reflected in the way National Curriculum for science is laid out. What I focus on in this next section of the chapter is creativity within the process of scientificstigation

The process of being a scientist, begins with asking questions - the 'what if' and 'why' which is at the core of creative thinking - and investigating possible answers to them by planning experiments, obtaining and considering evidence. Turning an idea into a question to ask, is the beginning of any investigation.

After finding a question to ask, the rest of the process of planning an experiment or investigation, involves:

* Making predictions
* Deciding how to test these
* Making a 'fair test'
* Deciding how to observe
* Measuring and recording
* Deciding what conclusions can be drawn from the results of the investigation
* Communicating the results

And the end of the process will involve children deciding what new investigations they might want to do. Having said this, the process presented above is an 'educator construct', and children do not always complete all parts of it on all occasions!

All science begins with observation: of phenomena, or properties, of a living being, a process, or an inanimate object. So enabling children to be scientists starts with providing plenty of opportunities for them to observe phenomena or properties, both within the classroom and outside of it. CDRom technology now allows a great deal to be brought in to the classroom, on which some observations, if not always investigations, can be based.

Helping children to find questions to ask

Helping children to think of questions which *they* want to find out the answers to, is important. They will find it easier and more meaningful to try and find out the answers to them if they themselves have asked the questions.

One way of helping children find the questions they want to ask is by asking them questions. Questions which are closely tied to what the children are already thinking are most helpful. The important thing is to develop the children's confidence in their own ideas - and using open questions can help in this.

'Open' questions have lots of possible answers, not just one correct one. They often begin with 'Why' or 'What' or 'How'. For example, 'How can you tell if these things are living?' or 'Why do apples have pips?' or 'How does the dough change when it goes in the oven?'. Open questions allow children to voice their own ideas. They also allow you to hear what the children have noticed, and what they consider important. Open questions also encourage children to get involved in the process of investigation.

On the other hand, 'closed' questions are ones where there is one correct answer. These questions often have a 'Yes' or 'No' answer, or a specific place, description, name or time. They often begin with words like 'Where' or 'When' or 'Is it'. For example, 'Where is your knee?' or 'When does chocolate melt?' or 'Is the light bulb on?'

In scientific investigation and experimentation, you need to use both open and closed questions. Closed questions can help children to observe what is happening. Open questions can help them to work out why that is.

Inevitably, if you are genuinely encouraging children to ask their own questions, they may come up with ones which are impossible to investigate in the classroom (although if you had a science laboratory with specialised equipment it might be possible). Some questions may even be impossible to find an answer to at all! So the discourse of science investigations needs to include recognition of what is and what is not possible to follow through in the classroom, whether you are working with three year olds or thirteen year olds. Another strategy is to create structured opportunities for children to ask scientific questions . The next step from creating the questions, is for the children to decide which ones are testable, and how to test them. This means making predictions.

Making predictions

You can help young children to make predictions by asking them questions about their investigations. The questions should encourage them to think *what* might happen, not why. The more the children can visualise what might happen, the better able they will be to test out their predictions. Each activity will produce a slightly different mix of reasons for predicting. One of the challenges can be to encourage the children to notice something about their investigation which might help them to predict.

What about the rest of the process of investigation?

I have focused so far on asking questions and making predictions, because they are perhaps the most creative part of the process of being a scientist. This is not to say that the other aspects of the process are un-creative. Adopting an atmosphere of conjecture, and by valuing more than one possibility at any stage, whether it is deciding on a way of both testing a hypothesis, and interpreting the results of a test, is a way of maintaining creativity throughout an investigation.

Deciding how to test predictions

Children's ideas about how to test their predictions will usually involve trying out them out. A key skill in testing scientific predictions, which most children will develop in their Junior years at school, is the idea of a fair test. The National Curriculum for Key Stage 1 also specifies that children should be taught to recognise when a comparison or a test is fair or unfair.

To make a fair test, the children need to have worked out the relevant, independent, dependent and control variables. Young children however will need lots of help to work out that a fair test is needed, and how to set one up. Few children in Key Stage 1 will be able to cope with the idea of a fair test. Although the thinking involved in devising a fair test may involve convergent, logical, thinking, the notion of 'possibility' is at its core. Occasionally too a divergent idea can contribute to devising the fair test.

A creative approach to fostering fair testing is one which enables all children to feel their ideas are valued, although eventually the only ones which will be chosen will be those which provide a genuine 'fair test'. There is an inevitable tension between accepting all ideas and deciding upon the most appropriate one; similar to that involved in 'brainstorming' where all ideas are accepted initially, but later they are sifted and a smaller number chosen, on the basis of some shared criteria.

Observation

Science observation involves focusing attention on to factual detail and is supported by questions like 'what can you see', 'what do you notice', 'what do you find inside/outside', 'what do you feel, see, hear,, taste', 'how many, how long, how often'. Observation is also more sharply focused by comparison questions - eg 'in how many ways are your leaves alike and how do they differ'.

Part of the process of becoming a scientist is being able to choose appropriate ways of observing, since science provides a pre-specified way of looking at things. Thus by 'modelling' the kinds of questions the children might ask is important. Although the questions are therefore constrained I would suggest they have at their core the 'what if' of possibility thinking.

Measuring and recording

Measuring will not be part of every investigation. For example, if children are investigating simple properties of different materials by exploring their textures, appearance, transparency and whether they are magnetic or non-magnetic, they may not need to measure anything. But if they are finding out what happens when water is heated or cooled, they will need to find a way of measuring what is applied to the water and how it responds. Helping children decide what to measure with involves supporting them in *learning what each kind of measuring instrument can do.*

Measuring instruments which young children might use in science will include ones which they have created for themselves. For instance, in an investigation into the conditions under which seeds grow, the children may devise their own forms of ruler (made up, for example, of finger-widths, Unifix cubes, or from squared paper). Children can sometimes find ways of using their measuring instruments which would not have occurred to you as the adult. This is another aspect of creativity within science.

Discussions about how and what they are measuring will reveal the children's ideas about what the measuring instrument is capable of. This can provide you with opportunities to extend the children's understanding - and to stimulate their creativity.

Recording the outcomes of a science investigation can involve creativity. There are a variety of different ways of recording work from a science investigation. They include drawing, annotated drawings, log books or diaries, writing, creating a bar chart, a graph or a table of results, and even talking in to a tape recorder. Children's personal recordings, in the form of diagrams, notes, spider charts and networks, can help them and you to to see each child's connections between the ideas.

Summing up on maths and science

Essentially both maths and science involve
* posing questions and exploring answers to them
* having access to domain-specific knowledge and concepts in order to do so.

Both involve what is called 'deductive' reasoning (which goes something like this: 'because this has happened I presume that the actions which led to it had such-and-such-a-function'). Both involve prediction, based on a body of knowledge. Perhaps because of this, many teachers don't consider these parts of the school curriculum to be creative. However both involve coming to new understandings and each has its own language which represents thinking. Both require creativity in that they demand that questions are asked, such as 'what if?'...

How can a computer be creative?

The games which are available for computers, the differentiated learning activities where children can monitor their own levels of achievement particularly on basic skills like reading or even key board skills, and some of the open ended investigations which are available are all ways in which children's creativity can be enhanced by computers.

But I would argue that the most powerful contribution that computers make to learning is through communications.

As I write this chapter, one of my colleagues at The Open University is visiting the School of Education in Milton Keynes, on research leave from his own university in Wagga Wagga, New South Wales, Australia. He is researching in a primary school there, and also in one in England. Since he is the common link, he has encouraged children in both schools to write to one another, but not using pencil and paper. Instead, the children send each other messages through electronic mail! The children in Australia also send messages to him, whilst he is here in England. The communication is thus inter-generational and inter-cultural too; the children have lots of questions about what he is doing on his visit, what he has seen and who he has met. If it weren't for the time difference between the two countries, the children and my colleague could talk to each other in 'real time' rather than waiting until the next day for a response to their messages. Instead, they chat through electronic mail waiting a day or so at a time to get a response to each previous comment or question.

So, computers provide a technology for fostering relationships in new ways, and transcending geographical and cultural boundaries. And they also provide a source of and a tool for manipulating, information, as Hammond has argued (1988). Take, for example, spreadsheets. A spreadsheet allows you to make calculations very fast in order to model possible outcomes as variables are altered. For example, when I am working out how much it will cost to produce an Open University course, I have to think about various different costs: the writing costs if we use a consultant, the editing, the design, the printing, the warehousing, the postage and distribution. Each of these costs varies with the amount of material involved. So, for each additional page, it costs more to write, edit and design. But printing in bulk costs much less per page than printing a small quantity. And of course that is just the print - I haven't talked about video, audio cassettes, CDRoms - etc. So my calculations are quite complicated. If I want to work out what I should charge students to study the course, I need to build in other costs, such as staff time for briefing and looking after tutors, tutor time for teaching the course face to face, and so on. Rather than having to work all of the possible variations out by hand, I can create a spreadsheet. What is really exciting about spreadsheets is that as the user, you are in charge of how they make the calculations! So, I can make up a plan for my spreadsheet to multiply, for example, the unit cost of each page of editing, by the number of pages which I anticipate, and to multiply the unit cost of design per page to the number of pages which I anticipate, and so on - and to add all of the outcomes together at the end. Making up the algebraic equations which drives that function is a very creative process: there are a often number of different equations each of which refers to a different part of the production process. So I need to develop an equation which will find out the total cost of each item, and then an overarching one which will total all of the functions at the end. Children, by the top end of junior school, are quite capable of setting up spreadsheets for their own purposes.

Adventure games provide another set of possibilities for children because although the worlds which they can explore are in fact pre-determined by the programme, they are often very complex, with events, characters, problems to be solved, and some kind of 'quest'. These kinds of games can provide stimulus for imagination at all kinds of levels. Some games are presented as simulations, such as diving in to retrieve a Tudor shipwreck, or having conversations with Egyptian priests in order to identify an object found on an archaeological dig. Of course, there are problems with the assumptions which can be implied by such simulations, as Scaife and Wellington (1993) point out: in real life the variables cannot be controlled

with such ease, so the picture presented can be misleading. In addition, it is possible of course as with all accounts, to come across biased CDRom presentations which on the face of it close down creativity. But given a critically reflective environment biased accounts can be used to stimulate creative responses in children.

Another creative capability which computers can help develop is the use of control technology through robots and programmes such as LOGO. The children can actually make up the instructions which control the movement of the turtle, robot or whatever. In this way computers become what Turkle and Papert call tools to think with (1990).

Another way in which computers can engage with individual creativity, as Loveless (1995) has pointed out, is their ability to present data in wide variety of ways, including using sound, sight, colour and movement. Cartoon-like animation and also being able to display information at the touch of a button in the form of graphs and charts, as well as in the form of 3-D models, means that children whose dominant learning styles need information in visual, auditory or modelled form, are much better provided for. Because the child controls the pace, there is scope for stretching each child's cognitive abilities.

So, how straightward *is* the accessing of information through computers?

Accessing non-linear information

Computer-aided learning often involves accessing information in an order which is selected by the learner. You may have observed children using CD-Rom disks of encycopaedias, or museums, for example. The child can decide what they want to find out about, and in what order. They can also decide how they want to find out (ie through screen text, on-screen video, computer audio or through the graphics, or a combination of all). The introduction of this kind of choice is extremely significant, as many researchers on both sides of the Atlantic, are finding out. As CD-Rom in particular becomes a more widespread medium for storing a variety of information (sound, images, text), the assumption that a user can find their way through a non-linear menu of possibilities will become a natural part of the expectations on young children for learning, both in school and at home. And as the Internet and WWW become more available to the general public, including children, this need for non-linear processing skills will increase.

Non-linear information contrasts with linear information where the order of presentation is much more pre-defined. Linear information may include more than one form of material (eg story tapes, or for adult learners, Open University style materials). The point is that the actual process of accessing non-linear information offers plenty more opportunities for creative thinking, than information which is presented in linear form.

Consider this example:

Alan and Christine are both class teachers in the same primary school, which provides each classroom with two computers, some of which have CD-Rom facilities. They have, however, very different approaches to learning with information technology.

Christine, who is the IT co-ordinator, has a class of 32 children in Y5. She decided to use a CD-Rom package and a database programme as resources for the children in exploring Tudor England. The children worked in threes and worked on the computer in timetabled slots throughout the day. She organised the history topic in two halves. In the first half, she provided the children with some information about the topic, through:

* the CD-Rom which the children could search themselves
* a dramatic play during one assembly (by a local theatre-in-education style group),
* a visit to a local museum,
* a variety of source books borrowed from a local library,
* some direct teaching in the classroom.

As they gathered information she asked the children to work in a variety of ways to identify questions

which they wished to know answers to, about the period under study.

In the second half of the history topic, the children were to find out answers to a variety of questions agreed by the class. She also added a few of her own. The resources included the CD-Rom, further library searches and also the database.

Alan, on the other hand, teaches 33 children in Y6. Although the children are even more capable of the kind of work Christine's class were undertaking, he is not keen on computers. Since Christine works with his class once a fortnight for an afternoon whilst he takes her class for maths, he tends to leave the IT to her. In contrast he teaches The Victorians from a text book, which both defines and answers the questions which might be asked about that era. As the book was published after the most recent National Curriculum Orders and there are enough for the children to share one between two, he sees no problem in working through it chapter by chapter on a Tuesday afternoon.

As teachers we need to be aware of what the medium of instruction expects of the child. This argument is made by an American review team (Alexander, Kulikowitch and Jetton, 1994) who published a summary of sixty-six studies by diverse researchers in education in this arena. I would argue that we also need to be aware of what opportunities are offered by each medium, for problem finding, and problem solving. The more scope there is for a child to define their own questions, the more scope the medium offers for creativity.

Of course, we need to be aware of potential barriers which can exist for both children and teachers, in using information technology: as well as the skills of being able to decode non-linear information as discussed earlier, some people do find it impersonal, and even, as Alan in the case study above puts it, 'irrelevant'! And there is also evidence that gender may play a part in how accessible the technology actually is (Spender, 1995).

Computers can on the other hand offer access to people

who have found it difficult to learn through linear and word-based models; for example dyslexics. For example, there are now computer programmes which operating on voice-recognition, can help someone who simply cannot read or write with any fluency, to write on to the screen. And as Tom West's work suggests (1991), computers can offer alternative ways of representing complex issues through three-dimensional, visual, models.

Finally, computers can of course mimic art, in that it is possible to paint and draw using them, investigating and trying out many possibilities in a way which is not possible when using the 'wet' materials.

Authenticity

There is increasing evidence that a vital aspect of effective learning activities is that they are authentic (ie meaningful) for pupils. This is one reason why communicating through electronic mail works as a creative learning medium for some people - they genuinely want to find out what is happening in someone else's life, or to hear about someone else's ideas.

But learning needs to be authentic in the sense of being situated within a subject area, too. Because learning in any part of the curriculum involves to some extent at any rate, what Clayden et al (1994) call 'enculturation' - or learning the culture, of a particular domain. One implication for teaching and learning is that children need clear and explicit access to the subjects of the curriculum themselves and not just to their packaging. So, children need access to the culture of the information stored on the hard disk, floppy disks and CD-Roms, just as they need access to the culture and 'rules' of reading books. AND they also need access to the culture of the subject about which the computer programme, game, etc. is about.

This means that teachers need a good knowledge of the 'culture' of a domain of knowledge in order to assess and plan children's learning so that it is authentic. So, Christine needed a good knowledge of the culture of the domain of history and historical study, in the example given above. Alan put a lot of trust in the text book to provide an appropriate model for using and interpreting evidence. By relying on the text book alone, Alan simplified his own preparation and thinking. On the other hand he offered the children fewer opportunities to explore authentic aspects of the subject, and limited the extent to which they could practice the skills of the historian. There were also few opportunities for creative, generative, thinking.

Design and technology

At the core of design and technology is the need for children to think creatively: to experiment, to be open to possibility, to take risks, to be prepared to combine old ways of seeing with new ones, to be prepared to look at a situation or problem in different ways, to seek innovation, to be resourceful. And it requires both 'right and left brain thinking' - introduced in chapter 1. In other words, design and technology requires both intuition, spatial orientation, crafts, skills, emotions, expression (all right hemisphere operations) and also language, sequencing, logic, mathematical operations. It is important to give children space to access the right hemisphere's functions, by offering opportunities to generate and clarify ideas through working together, through drama, discussion, also modelling, sketching, painting, working with construction kits, and through information technology drawing and designing packages.

From their research into design and technology in schools, the Assessment of Performance Unit (APU, 1991 and SEAC, 1991) have concluded that key elements are active capability and reflective capability. Cross (1994) has developed these to include creative capability:

Active capability: *constructive thinking, doing, action*
Reflective capability: *evaluating, review*
Creative capability: *imagination, invention; including aesthetic and technological creativity*

      Source: Cross (1994), p19

Children's ideas can be stimulated by what the Design and Technology in Education Project (1990) has called 'design awareness' - which means experiencing and engaging critically with the made world of places, products and images. As Tickle (1990) has said, 'the problem faced by the teacher is how to stimulate and guide without imposing too many preconceptions and stereotypes, and without stifling the child's own creativity and logical thinking and making' (p112). Thus the issue is how to provide possibilities for children's thinking without pre-constraining their frameworks of reference.

In this sense, design and technology requires teachers to exercise their imaginations, as others have argued (Ritchie, 1995). The provision of authentic starting points and background contexts for children requires designing the curriculum and activities in a way which allows for many possibilities. Drawing on contexts and experiences which are meaningful to the children involves possibility thinking on the part of the teacher. Clearly, children can potentially play a role in identifying meaningful starting points for investigations. Consider the case of Helen.

Helen teaches Y6 in an inner city school in Newcastle-upon-Tyne. She has a policy of seeking children's interests and conceptions at the start of each project of work. Recently the children were undertaking a history project based around the Newcastle Quayside (a historic dockside area which has now become a bijoux place full of craft shops, tea rooms, restaurants and wine bars). As a starting point she asked the children to work first individually and then in small groups to brainstorm and then 'concept map' what they knew about the Quayside,

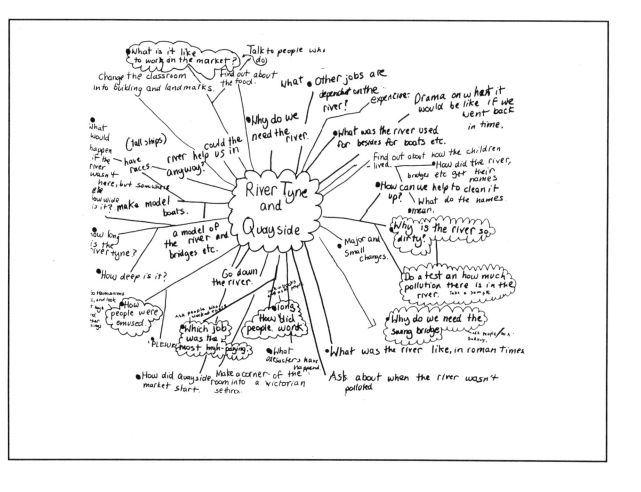

and what questions arose for them about it. This is one of them.

The children reported back to one another in a variety of ways, and from the discussions which followed, Helen was able to plan a range of potential starting points for the children. Her expectation, shared explicitly with the children, was that as their interests developed so too might the topic, in the way that Bob Jeffrey describes trail following, in Chapter 5.

Helen's work illustrates two points. First, that opportunities for design and technology exist in lots of curriculum areas and topic focused themes; they also exist in the day to day life of the classroom, as the list suggested by Cross (1994) illustrates: 'for example, the storage of coats; the care of pets; the storage of resources; the transport of materials; the library; the gardens and grounds; jobs done in school, etc'. Other sources of starting points include the media and children's fiction.

Helen's work illustrates secondly that finding out the children's perspectives on what is relevant is important and possible.

Authenticity

Authenticity in design and technology is an issue facing both curriculum designers at policy level, and also classroom teachers. As Siraj-Blatchford (1996) and others (APU 1993) have argued, The National Curriculum for design and technology describes a linear model where each stage is clearly defined and distinct from the next. The actual complex realities of the process of designing, making and evaluating are actually ignored. Indeed, in the initial version of the National Curriculum for design and technology, even the numbering of the attainment targets implied that there was a natural starting point ("Identification of Needs and Opportunities") which is often not the actual place where the design and technology process starts. The linear model is also too difficult for children who are very young or who have very little experience. Identifying a need, or a 'problem' to be solved, requires powers of analysis which, like the creativity required for the design process, do not necessarily spring 'naturally' from within, but rather, need practice in the form of experience and examples from more experienced designers.

Having a 'model' of what is involved in design and technology in your head is, like in any curriculum area, important if you are to plan and assess learning. Ideally, models of the process involved in design and technology should involve childen in finding a variety of design solutions to problems which are, increasingly with age and experience, identified by them. But in practice, the problem with such models (including the National Curriculum one) is that the approach can become formulaic and artificial. It can stifle creativity because children look for the right answer rather than the optimum solution. And it can make the process of designing and making appear to be smooth and clear. In fact as the APU's research (APU, 1991 and SEAC, 1991) carried out between 1985 and 1991 suggests, the process is muddled - children seem to generate ideas and try them out without formal design stages, and they seem to focus on the detail of their ideas. The APU and others (Cross, 1994) describe a seeming muddle of to-ing and fro-ing between the mind and the hand, or between active and reflective work as a natural part of the process.

Oversimplification may lead on to another problem: what both teacher and children think 'counts'. McCormick and Davidson (1996) describe research work with children aged 11 - 14 in which they discovered the teacher actually rated neat work which did not function in practice, over less tidy work which actually did function! This often led to children aiming to please the teacher by producing neat diagrams and drawings, but non-functional designs!

Designing technologies for a creative future?

Clearly, to some extent, design and technology involves creativity, as it is about children realising their own creations. They must use creative forms of expression, such as drawing and other modelling techniques, to explore their thoughts. As Siraj-Blatchford (1996) points out, playing, too, can usefully be used as a process to support design and technology. Drawing on Pepler's (1982) classification of theories of play, it can *enable children to explore their environment*, it can provide opportunities for them to experiment, in other words to go beyond what any object or phenomenon can do, *to find out what they can do with it*. And finally play can *help children to think abstractly,* as play objects are representational of the 'real' world.

A driving force, of course, behind design and technology, is that the solution should 'work'. De Bono (1982) emphasises in his writing about divergent thinking, that a way of evaluating the success of an idea is the extent to which it works. But I want to add an ethical dimension also. At all kinds of levels, children are the next guardians of our globe. The ideas which they have about what to design and make in it, will have environmental, economic, social and spiritual impact in the world. It is important that children's ideas work, but more importantly than that, it seems to me, they need the opportunity to explore choices. As Einstein said, 'The problems that we face today cannot be solved with the same level of understanding we had when we created them'. As our society continues to value inventiveness and innovation, children need access not only to that process but also familiarity with a critical and ethical framework with which they can evaluate the potential impacts of their choices.

Acknowledgements

Thanks are due to my colleagues in The Open University School of Education, for informal conversations and drafting processes over the past six years, which have informed the writing of this chapter. I have also drawn on material and research for the maths section from the Centre for Mathematics Education in The Open University and for the science section on an early draft of my writing for the Open University's Specialist Teaching Assistants' Course (E660). Thanks also to John Siraj-Blatchford for his expert comments on the science and technology sections in particular.

Summing up on technology:

I have suggested that information technology provides several kinds of opportunity for fostering children's creativity, particularly in non-linear processing of information.

For design and technology in the classroom, as with maths and science, children also need to understand some of the physical properties of materials and tools, and ways of using them, in order to realise their ideas. Providing authentic learning experiences for children in design and technology depends on an accurate definition of the school curriculum for design and technology, and on teachers having an adequate understanding of criteria for supporting and assessing children's efforts. I have tried to demonstrate how design and technology provides opportunities for both finding and solving problems, and I have argued that part of a creative approach to design and technology means providing children with access to an ethical framework for evaluating possibilities.

Concluding thoughts on maths, science and technology

Einstein said,

'Imagination is more important than knowledge'.

I am of the view, as I hope I have demonstrated during this chapter, that in maths, science and technology, *both* imagination, *and* knowledge (including skill), are important for the children to whom we pass on our world.

References

Alexander, P.A., Kulikowich, J.M., Jetton, T. L. (1994), 'The role of subject-matter knowledge and interest in the processing of linear and non-linear texts', *Review of Educational Research,* New York, American Educational Research Association

Assessment of Performance Unit (APU) (1991), *The Assessment of Performance in Design and*

Technology, London: SEAC

Assessment of Performance Unit (APU) (1993), 'Learning Through Design and Technology', in McCormick, R. et al, *Teaching and Learning Technology,* Addison Wesley

de Bono, E. (1982), *de Bono's Thinking Course,* British Broadcasting Corporation

Briggs, M. (1989), *Perceptions of confidence: an investigation into primary mathematics co-ordinators' perceptions of their colleagues' confidence in teaching mathematics,* unpublished dissertation, MA in Curriculum Studies, University of London Institute of Education

Clayden, E., Desforges, C., Mills, C. and Rawson, W. (1994), 'Authentic activity and learning', *British Journal of Educational Studies,* vol. XXXXII, no. 2, June 1994, Oxford/Cambridge, Mass: Blackwell. Later reproduced in Craft, A. (ed) (1996), *Primary Education: Assessing and Planning Learning,* London: Routledge

Cross, A. (1994), *Design and Technology 5 - 11,* London: Hodder & Stoughton

Design and Technology in Education Project, (1990), *What is design?* Halifax: Design Dimension Educational Trust

Hammond, J. H. (1988), The Second Wave: Information Technology and Literacy, in Sendov, A.B., Stanchev, I. (1988), *Children in the Information Age: Opportunities for Creativity, Innovation and New Activities, Selected Papers from the Second International Conference, Sofia, Bulgaria 19-23 May 1987,* Oxford: Pergamon Press

Haylock, D., Cockburn, A. (1989), *Understanding Early Years Mathematics,* London: Paul Chapman Publishing

Loveless, A. (1995), *The Role of I.T.: Practical Issues for the Primary Teacher,* London: Cassell

McCormick, R. Davidson, M. (1996), 'Problem Solving and the Tyranny of Product Outcomes, *Journal of Design and Technology Education,* 1 (3), 230-241

Murphy, P., Scanlon, E. (1994), *PGCE Teaching in Primary Schools Primary Science Module 1,* Milton Keynes: The Open University

Pepler, D.J. (1982), Play and Divergent Thinking, in Pepler, D.J. and Rubin, K.H. (eds) (1982), *The Play of Children: Current theory and research,* London: S.Karger

Ritchie, R. (1995), *Primary Design and Technology: A Process for Learning,* London: David Fulton Publishers

Scaife, J. and Wellington, J. (1993), *Information Technology in Science and Technology Education,* Buckingham and Philadelphia: Open University Press

Schools Examination and Assessment Council (SEAC) (1991), *The Assessment of Performance in Design and Technology (Goldsmith's Project),* London: HMSO

Siraj-Blatchford, J. (1996), *Learning Technology, Science and Social Justice: an integrated approach for 3 - 13 year olds, An Education Now Handbook,* Nottingham: Education Now Publishing Co-operative

Spender, D. (1995), *Nattering on the Net,* Melbourne, Australia: Spinifex Press

Tickle, L. (ed) (1990), *Design and Technology in Primary School Classrooms,* Lewes: The Falmer Press

Turkle, S. and Papert, S. (1990), 'Epistemological pluralism: signs and voices within the computer culture', *Signs: Journal of Women in Culture and Society,* 16 (1)

West, T. (1991) *In the Mind's Eye: Visual Thinkers, Gifted People with Learning Difficulties, Computer Images, and the Ironies of Creativity,* Amherst, NY: Prometheus Books, Seventh Printing, July 1996

Part 3

Teachers developing their practice

Introduction

Part Three focuses on teachers developing their practice in enabling children's creativity. In Chapter 5, Bob Jeffrey focuses on teachers and their practice, suggesting ways in which to identify, describe and develop creative practice.

As touched on earlier in the book, the culture of both the classroom and wider community has an influence on specific pedagogic strategies and potentially too what is considered to be pupil creativity. Some of these ideas are explored in Chapter 6, where I draw in particular on observations from a small collaborative research project which I am working on with primary school teachers of English in Southern Spain.

In Chapter 7, I explore, with Tom Lyons, aspects of teacher nourishment, asking how teachers can nourish themselves in order to foster creativity in the classroom. We explore in particular the role of the non-conscious and how to enable that element of one's creativity to flow in to practice, and we draw on data from our research project with educators in South-East England.

Teaching as artistry is a strong theme in Part Three of the book, and I hope that teachers will find it both a useful reflection on their practice, as well as offering challenges for developing it in a variety of ways.

Anna Craft

Chapter 5

Framing Creativity in Primary Classrooms

Bob Jeffrey

School based activity, involving participative observation and inquiry can help in discovering, creating and supporting creative teaching.

In this chapter, I argue that creative practices have not only been marginalised by the current educational emphasis on the bureaucratic aspects of teaching and learning but that they have also been made invisible by teachers' isolated practices and their lack of interpretive frame, or perspectives, to appreciate each other's creativity. I suggest that there are opportunities within new supervisory, collaborative, mentoring and professional development practices for teachers to recover the acknowledgement of their artistry. Through the case study of a recent research project in which I was involved, I introduce a model of collaborative professional development in which teachers support one another in reflecting back, reflecting on and developing their classroom practice.

I suggest four interpretive frames on practice, which emerged through this project, and explore conversational strategies which formed part of the enquiry, with the intention that other teachers may find these useful. Though drawn from research in primary schools it is hoped that teachers across the 3-13 age range will find it of relevance.

The Current Climate and Creative Teaching

Primary schools have been swamped with 'knowledge, skills and understanding' via the National Curriculum. Other bureaucratic trends in recent years have resulted in moving the focus away from teacher creativity to form-filling for curriculum planning and assessment of learning (Woods and Jeffrey 1996). The latest introduction of OFSTED inspections has narrowed the

focus even more, in that classroom control and 'safe' teaching becomes the teacher's priority (Jeffrey and Woods 1995). One way in which teachers can maintain some control over practice as well as resisting the narrowing of focus, is to find time for the investigation and development of creative practices within new collaborative practices being established.

School based activity, involving participative observation and inquiry can help in discovering, creating and supporting creative teaching. With the 'cracking of the classroom walls of privatism' (Day 1993) in primary schools (through the processes of inspection and appraisal), it is expected that more people will be working in classrooms, observing and developing primary practice. Whilst some of this is purely evaluative, e.g. inspections and local 'audits', much of the rest can be turned to teachers advantage in terms of professional development and dialogue providing some frames are developed in each school as to how to do it. One opportunity, for example, might be through the development of monitoring. The vast majority of OFSTED reports on primary schools mention the need for subject monitoring by postholders, particularly the observation of fellow colleagues to assist with national curriculum and school policy implementation and although it may not have been taken up by many schools yet there is considerable pressure for them to implement it. Many of the teachers who should be doing this are not keen to 'monitor' but they do see a value in engaging with colleagues over discussions concerning their practice, for which there is less and less time to do so in the current climate (Woods at al, forthcoming). Other opportunities could include mentoring arrangements between students and teachers, and arrangements between class teachers and the qualified teachers and teaching assistants who support children in the classroom on a part time basis.

However, in making a shift toward the appreciation of creative teaching, one of the challenges is to convince many teachers of their own creativity. As Anna Craft indicated in Chapter One, teaching is seen as a job that requires and involves fostering creativity, yet very few teachers, according to Fryer and Collings (1991) regard themselves as particularly creative, 'the most frequently selected attributes tended to be concerned with social attributes and willingness to work hard' (p 211). Is this because teachers are not inventive, imaginative and inspirational or might it be because teachers have had little opportunity either to observe other teachers' creativity or to value their own?

I would like to suggest that perhaps teachers do not credit their own creative acts because much of it goes unrecorded and therefore unrecognised. In spite of teachers regretting the diminution of spontaneity in terms of curriculum organisation (Pollard et al 1994 pp 85] there are still many spontaneous acts relating to specific activities in teachers' classrooms. Much of this action, because of its spontaneous nature, is unrecorded and therefore does not achieve status in a discourse (like that of OFSTED) which is trying to establish uniformity (Jeffrey and Woods, forthcoming).

Creative Teaching

Creative teaching in the primary school involves innovation, ownership, control and relevance, (Woods 1990). This may involve in any given situation some or all of these features, an innovative idea or approach, some ownership and control over the process by the teacher and the pupil, and the event must be relevant to both teacher and pupil. Creative teaching has been identified in a number of different contexts, for example, a first school committed to environmental and community involvement, the making of a film about a village life, the involvement of children in planning a new town hall (Woods 1995). Creative teaching has been seen being used in topics about the solar system, maths programmes and historical investigations. Creative teaching involves consideration of the emotions, the creation of tone and atmosphere, the recognition of the importance of narrative for children and a critical approach to knowledge (Woods and Jeffrey 1996). At the centre of the creative process is the teacher who artfully develops pupil's learning experiences. For Eisner, (1979) educational improvement comes not from the discovery of scientific methods that can be applied universally, or from particular personalities, but 'rather from enabling teachers...to improve their ability to see

and think about what they do' (p.104), or in other words, their 'art of appreciation', a subtle ability to discriminate. (Woods and Jeffrey 1996 p. 3)

Creative teaching is also effective because every situation is different. A multiplicity of factors affect the teaching moment involving such shifting elements as the state of knowledge, space and time, cultural considerations, resources, human capacity and predilection. As Dewey (1929, p.6) notes,

'Judgement and belief regarding actions to be performed can never attain more than a precarious probability.....Practical activity deals with individualized and unique situations which are never exactly duplicable and about which, accordingly, no complete assurance is possible'

Only so much is predictable. There is a need, therefore, for teachers to be flexible. It is not a matter of having certain fixed solutions that can be applied to certain fixed problems; nor of reflecting on the possibilities and making a conscious decision about which combination of actions to take. Rather, skill and judgement are required in selecting from and applying existing knowledge in what Schon (1983) calls 'knowledge-in-action'. Much of this is embedded deep within the teacher's subconscious, and operated intuitively. Teachers may find it difficult to articulate in words the reasons for their actions, but this is typical of artistic accomplishments (Hargreaves, 1983).

However, if school based research into creative teaching is to become a feature of a school's professional development then participants will also need some frames which enable them to see the creative teaching that many teachers fail to recognise as part of their practice. Indicators of creative teaching - innovation, control, ownership and relevance - have been identified by detailed research which used and developed various frames through which the teaching and learning process was scrutinised (Woods, 1990). These frames, like the frames of a film, are selective shots that allow the observer an opportunity to appreciate the content of a specific context.

Summing up so far:

I have suggested that:

* many primary schools have become bureaucratised through changes in curriculum, assessment, resourcing and accountability (including inspection), nevertheless

* strategies such as peer observation, introduced through inspection reports, can be turned to the advantage of teachers and schools by offering opportunities to identify creative teaching,

* among the challenges in doing so is convincing teachers that their practice may be creative, ie recognising it, as much creative teaching goes unrecorded and unacknowledged.

In the next part of the chapter I look at some aspects of creative teaching.

Creativity Frames

There are, according to Eisner (1979), multiple ways in which the teaching in a classroom can be viewed or known. An artist and a scientist will describe a teacher's work differently as human knowledge is a reflection of the mind as well as of the situation one observes.

The forms through which people represent their conception of the world have a major influence on what they are able to say. So, in observing a teacher's practice for creative events, the observer must decide what he or she will be sensitive to and they must be appreciative of creative possibilities.

An OFSTED inspection appears to limit its focus to those designated items in the OFSTED Handbook (OFSTED 1996) and uses an evaluative approach which is less to do with appreciation than with numerical standardisation. Observation of creative practices is an appreciation of qualities, those aspects of the practice that are germane to the situation. Observers - and these can be the teachers themselves

as well as other classroom workers - can become educational connoisseurs (Eisner 1979). Like wine connoisseurs they can learn how to appreciate the qualities of a teacher's work - they develop 'frames' through which to explore the teacher's practice.

During a recent research project which focused on creative teaching, we (Woods and Jeffrey 1996) established four such frames. The research looked at the work of five primary teachers in depth over 2-3 terms using observational field notes, recorded conversations and general engagement (i.e. informal meetings, discussions with teachers, support at children's performances and some classroom assistance). In this chapter, I focus on the engagement between Judy, a teacher, and myself, Bob, the researcher.

At the time of the research Judy was in her late forties, had returned to teaching some five years earlier and was teaching year 2 and 3 in a small one form entry school in inner London. I had taught in primary schools for over twenty years, after which he took up a university based research post investigating creative teaching through ethnographic methods.

Judy and I engaged in conversations ranging across politics, biographies, learning strategies, academic work (Judy was in the middle of studying for her MA) and school issues. We met mainly in cafes and chatted for hours. Judy was given copies of any papers that were produced and invited to comment. Much of this is similar to a Mutual Support and Observation (M.S.O.) project (Gates 1989) where secondary teachers observed each other and discussed their observations and perspectives. In this way we developed a 'third eye', which began to give us insight into our own actions; a form of standing outside oneself (Gates 1989 pp 34).

We constructed ideas and understandings as we talked (Jeffrey 1995). However, I was not the researcher teacher and she was not the teacher researcher (Woods and Wenham 1995). I was the participative researcher though I did assist in the class and Judy was the participative teacher interested in engaging with me in research and dialogue. I found four frames, in particular, useful for the development of our discussions about creative practice. They are:

* inspired actions,
* the generation of atmospheres,
* knowledge engagement and
* negotiative approaches.

Frame 1: Inspired Actions

Nearly fifty percent of the teachers in the Fryer and Collings research (1991) thought creativity involved inspiration. The most frequent spontaneous events quoted by teachers (Woods and Jeffrey 1996) are ones where the curriculum focus changes for a significant amount of time, for example, children bringing a bird's nest into school or the hatching out of frogs in the school pond. However, inspired actions are distinct from purely spontaneous ones, in that they are mainly concerned with a teacher making use of inspiration to develop her current curriculum focus.

Judy spontaneously picked on a melon (which Bob had brought in for the children as a thank you present, for helping him with the research), to revise their knowledge about the 'worlds' topic they had been pursuing. She encouraged the children to allocate to each planet in our solar system a fruit symbol, e.g.: strawberry for the smallest and the melon for the largest.

These opportunistic features of teaching reflect for children a more 'poetic' way of thinking, one in which the learner 'works along with' phenomena as opposed to a 'calculative rational' approach where the learner 'works upon' the phenomenon and attempts to control it (Bonnett 1994 p 130). The frequent use of inspired actions may also indicate to the child the extent of the value attached by teachers to a form of thinking which is less linear and more imaginative, again in keeping with their experiences as people who are inquisitive about their world and who are continually making connections for understanding and meaning.

While demonstrating how to do a mathematical transposition of a figure of a giant Judy realised that the children were becoming restless and she suddenly burst into a story about which planet her giant lived on, its clothes, characteristics and life related to the planet's climate and environment. She then engaged the children's imagination for a few minutes about their own giants before sending them off to complete the transposition. These inspired acts creatively enhance particular learning situations. They also lead to 'trail following'.

The teacher may not be quite sure where the trail will lead her but at the time it seems relevant to explore. Following trails is more concerned with an interruption in the flow of the classroom plans and may be used creatively or not. One afternoon a story read by Judy concerning pollution which related to the class topic, led to her tale of a miner, whom she knew, with silicosis. This led on to a debate amongst the children about smoking, which revealed that many of them didn't like the smoky atmospheres they were sometimes forced to experience.

In another incident Judy was describing the use of bleach for some science in which they were engaged and the swimming baths was mentioned as being a place where they might have encountered the smell. She let the children tell many stories of their experiences of the swimming baths, believing that by making personal connections between the baths and the chemical - analogy and application - the children would remember significantly more about bleach than if she had didactically given them information about it. Trails then, are possibilities which may lead to dead ends, but they allow the possibility for productive and effective learning.

Frame 2: Generation of Atmospheres

The generation of atmospheres is an important element in teaching and learning (Woods and Jeffrey 1996, Craft, 1997). In *Teachable Moments,* for example, Peter Woods and I (1996) identified three constructions of atmosphere which were particularly indicative of our teachers:

* the andante - moderately slow and serious,

* the legato - in other words, an even tempo, and

* the spiritoso - with spirit.

Teacher dominant class lessons characterised the first, a working atmosphere characterised the second and the third was one in which there was great excitement. The way atmospheres are generated in a primary classroom and how they are constructed is a subject that is, in our experience, rarely discussed by teachers and yet they do it all the time. Some teachers use a rhythmic, almost poetic way of talking, others use humour, warmth, quiet approaches and personal relations. Two of the secondary teachers in the Mutual Support and Observation project spent part of a Friday evening discussing a smile between one of the teachers and a pupil (Gates, 1989).

While each teacher may work in a particular way which reflects their personality and professional approach, there are nuances and subtleties that pervade their practice. In this chapter I am suggesting that debate or discussion about this aspect of a teacher's craft, or artistry, would encourage teachers to investigate more closely how they created their own classroom atmospheres and how this in itself was a creative activity.

Frame 3: Knowledge Engagement

There are a number of knowledges being expressed, experienced and considered in classrooms. Judy valued established knowledge, personal knowledge, possibility knowledge and at the same time she ensured that the constitution of knowledge was investigated by such activities as gathering evidence, argument and counter argument, and by developing critical faculties.

She showed how she valued established knowledge such as the anti-apartheid work of Nelson Mandela, or the scientific facts pertaining to the universe or the qualities of a good story by engaging the children in discussion about it.

"I wonder what's wrong with the earth? What do you think's happening?"

She encouraged 'possibilities' from children and

individual interpretations as a step in gaining an understanding of factual knowledge:

"there's another thing here that puzzles me a little bit. It's where it says 'the clouds that are fed with moisture from my forest no longer gather and rain cannot fall from them'. What does that mean?"

She doesn't ask for the answer but for an observation

"My tall forests are dying or being cut down so I can no longer breath properly. Put your hand up if you're going to tell me something about that"

Answers to general questions were not rejected. Instead she said 'I see' or 'let's see what someone else thinks'. In this way she allowed children in a group to reject their own answers privately, in favour of other answers that received commendation from the group or her.

However, she also showed how established knowledge could be examined by offering different perspectives such as a Hindu perspective on how the world is perceived - and incidentally fulfilled her Religious Education curriculum commitments. She encouraged the children either in groups or individually to offer opinions and possibilities as to how they thought these knowledges could be verified.

"Rosa says all the petrol from cars is going up in the sky and it makes the sky really horrible, we breathe it in. Can it really make the sky torn?'

In other classroom situations, groups of pupil investigators were quizzed by the rest of the class, about their processes, findings and conclusions, for example, during their investigation of the ratio of surface area and volume of some giant's utensils they had constructed. In this way knowledge was often only a 'possibility' until rigour in terms of belief or/ and scientific approaches had been exhausted.

Judy valued personal knowledge such as children's experiences of life - teeth pulling, smoking, bullying, imaginative stories - dreams, torture chambers, and other possibility knowledges, - 'the world might blow up tomorrow', 'there may be giants living under the sea' by allowing time and space (Gates 1989) and again encouraging debate amongst the children about the nature of these knowledges in terms of truth, speculation and opinion. The valuing of personal knowledge by her indicated to children the general value of knowledge in our society whereas the means by which she encouraged the children to engage in discussions about personal knowledge ensured the children learnt something about how to interrogate knowledge, about different forms of verification in science or through cultural and religious practices.

The approach, by teachers, to knowledge is fundamentally connected to what children actually learn about the nature of knowledge. All children 'know things' and they are interested in knowing more, but what they actually know about the various forms of knowledge partly comes from the way in which the teacher presents knowledge-framing (Bernstein 1977) and how she plays with knowledge. Knowledge investigation is the major focus of a classroom and how the teacher creatively engages with knowledge is a major part of her pedagogy, yet it is often only discussed narrowly by teachers in terms of classroom organisation and the extent of children's receptivity based in a delivery model of knowledge. By focusing on the detail of teachers' engagement with knowledge it is possible to highlight many of the different and creative ways aspects of their practice.

Frame 4: Negotiative Approaches

A particular context for creativity is the teacher's use of negotiability with the pupils. Like the other frames, this offers opportunities for the children in their choice of approach.

Judy negotiated with one child who wanted to work on the construction of a giant rather than do his maths by saying 'yes, OK but you will have to do it at a later session'. She nearly always said 'yes' rather than 'no' though she would often add a 'but....' which either offered a trade or a question relating to the consequences of the child's request and then let the child decide on his or her course of action. Proposals to alter the timetable or curriculum plans by the

children, e.g.: to go and see the frogs in the pond, were met with questions about how they could accommodate the original plans and the new proposals.

The constraints and possibilities were discussed by the children and new arrangements decided. During disputes between children, those involved and others were asked to offer suggestions as to how to resolve the issue. Developing the practice of negotiation in the classroom not only constructs processes in which children can engage and experience ways of working and relating but it develops the creative skills of pupils and teachers as they handle the negotiations. Some teachers may not work quite at the level of negotiation that Judy works but there will always be some areas of negotiation being exhibited, for example, over resources.

Any observation or self reflection concerning negotiation, however small, could be the first step to expanding the area of negotiation and analysing its usefulness. It may also lead to involving the pupils in evaluating classroom practices. It is quite clear that even primary pupils have insightful evaluations as to the value of creative approaches (Jeffrey and Woods 1997).

Summary of the four frames:

In this section of the chapter I have suggested that:

* creative teaching in the primary classroom involves innovation, ownership, control and relevance, all identified by Woods (1990), and

* creative teaching is complex, artful and flexible.

By drawing on a case study of some research which I carried out in collaboration with a teacher, Judy, I have identified four 'frames' for describing or 'viewing' aspects of her creative teaching:

* inspired actions,
* generation of atmospheres,
* knowledge engagement, and
* negotiative approaches.

I have contrasted the evolutionary and generative methodology which Judy and I adopted in order to come up with the four frames, with the designated and evaluative items specified by OFSTED.

The four frames outlined here are not exclusive but cover a good deal of a primary teachers' practice. They are as I have indicated in the summary above, also frames where the teacher has a significant degree of choice - a necessary condition for creativity. They can lead not only to the identification of creative practices but to the development of those practices.

So, what might the process of investigating and talking about the results of these observations look like?

Investigation and Conversation Strategies

There were three relevant aspects to my research involvement with Judy.

Firstly, I recorded in written notes everything that I thought might be significant in a chronological order. Secondly, at the same time I let my imagination work on the notes and added various insights or questions at the side of the chronological notes. I was also alert to new frames through which I might perceive creativity in action and the ones suggested in the last section are some of those that emerged from that imaginative process. In the same way other observers may construct new frames or characteristics of creativity as they observe and converse with other teachers or adults.

Thirdly, we engaged in conversations about the classroom practices. It may not be possible for a support teacher to do all these in detail while she is engaged with other classroom activities but a few observations during her time in the classroom could generate further discussion. If a teacher was doing this on their own they would obviously have to make their own notes and then engage a colleague in discussion later. I will now explore four different aspects of our conversations:
* asking questions,
* offering analysis,
* making assertions, and
* being controversial.

Asking Questions

I asked Judy about how she engaged her professional judgement as in this example concerning extra help given to a child through dance therapy,

So how has this arisen? Would you have sat down and said 'I've got an idea of what she's like, I think this would do her some good'... Have you got a tick checklist of things and as problems arise you find one that suits her? Or does it work more spontaneously, somebody happens to mention dance and you think, 'I know, Kathleen can do with that?'

In this case she was clear about why she had made that decision.

'No, no we're aware of the value of dance because we've seen what dance has done for the children'.

In other circumstances she developed her analysis through the conversation in response to a fundamental question, as this extract indicates.

***Judy** Quite often, for young children the frustration of being a young child is not having the skills to develop things in art and creative work and they have wonderful visions as children, beautiful visions, but they don't have the skills to produce them and I just like us to be able to give them the chance.*

***Bob** Is that what learning is?*

***Judy** Possibly, it's got to be hasn't it? I mean acquiring the skills but without losing the vision. This is what we do quite often. I don't know, maybe teachers impose their own vision but the children need to develop their visions for it is central to get them thinking creatively.*

An interpretation of her practice emerges from a conversation where she is faced with defining her own practice. The creativity involved in her practice is due to the balancing, in this case, of the vision and the skills.

In other circumstances my analysis was the basis for appreciation.

Offering Analysis

In some cases Judy had not perceived of the situation as I did, as the following extract shows.

Bob   There's a 'non fault syndrome' where you avoid describing children as at fault. You look for something else, that maybe they 'forgot'. So a child is able to say, for example 'what was wrong was the forgetting, not me'. You put the fault somewhere else, not on to the person but something that may be connected to the person which they can see outside themselves - the other, it's the other and not the I, if you like.

Judy   I hadn't thought of it like that actually.

Or I noticed things that were unusual and re-used classroom language to describe them:

Bob   Apart from giving them a 'have a go' writing book you encourage a 'have a go' approach to maths and science as well.

Judy   It's because they're thinking it through. It's much more valuable than me giving them too many clues because what I would be saying is 'I know something and I want you to guess what it is', which is really pseudo questioning. It's very painful, this thinking business, isn't it. They have to keep coming for reassurance and they're perplexed and puzzled. Quite a lot of people might think, 'oh well this teacher has not planned this activity and has not given the children the information in order for them to complete the task', but in fact, the task is thinking about something and working something out and trying to deduce something. If they're simply given a load of information that makes it quite obvious that they have to do it, they're taking on what somebody tells them and they're just fulfilling a task, they're factory operatives.

Making Assertions

At other times I would make assertions as in any conversation, but ones which were rooted in the current discourse and in the case which follows, Judy expands on the assertion from her own point of view.

Bob   What seems to be significant about knowledge and stories and reading is that children get their hands straight on to 'the knowledge'. It hasn't come from the teacher and if they have the choice then they can take it or leave it and consequently feel in control.

Judy   And it does becomes theirs, especially if they're not able to read all the text for they make their own stories from the pictures but they're still taking the stories from that book.

In this case Judy developed the assertion but at other times she also rejected assertions and substituted other interpretations which led to further analysis and speculation.

Bob   I've got evidence to show you using imagination in conversations and how it relates to established knowledge.

Judy   Actually, I don't think I'm doing enough to educate the imagination in children because in order to do this you've got to be open ended.

As the discussion developed I had used some of my observations to show she was more open-ended than she imagined. This appreciative approach made her think more closely about her practice.

I also pursued controversial issues whenever I thought it was relevant.

Being Controversial

Bob   People would generally suggest that children can't deal with morality and we have to teach them morality. You seem to be suggesting that they do make judgements.

Judy: Yes, all the time, of course. They make judgements as they're learning to speak and to think. As they're taking on board language and understanding they're taking on board notions of pain and pleasure, and good and bad, they're taking on board all those ideas. In any discussion with children, even children in the nursery you can have discussions on morality. I mean discussions on who did what to whom and why. They're all moral judgements that they're making.

Summary of investigation and conversation strategies

By drawing on the case study of the collaborative research investigating Judy's practice, I identified three elements which formed part of the investigation process :
* making chronological notes of anything which might be relevant,
* thinking imaginatively about the notes, adding insights and questions at the side of the notes; this included potential 'frames' to describe her practice, and
* numerous conversations with Judy about classroom practice.

I have explored four aspects of our conversations, giving examples to illustrate each:
* asking questions,
* offering analysis,
* making assertions and
* being controversial.

In this way I have sought to offer an insight in to how we 'constructed the conversations' (Jeffrey 1995) and consequently uncovered more of Judy's creative practice. In many instances the teacher may not have even thought about some of the areas we discussed and the ensuing conversations were a development of a new way of viewing her practice. In this approach we slid easily between her conscious intentions and new constructions of how her practice could be perceived. Moreover, we re-defined some of her practice in terms that were our own. Apart from claiming some ownership of the practice we were also able to elaborate the nature of the creative practice in terms of our values.

Conclusion

One of the consequences of more school based research of the kind described here is that teachers and observers or participant engagers can take joint ownership of some of their own creative findings as we did.

Judy encouraged different starting times for pupils entering new project work (Woods and Jeffrey 1996). Some children began investigating the class topic some two or three weeks ahead of other children. This had the advantage of allowing the less confident pupils to observe the development of the project and to build on already established structures in a 'scaffolded' manner before they entered the project. Those who had begun the project first - early entries - were then allowed to consider their early attempts and to alter them in the light of the general development of the project within the class so they built on their work in more depth. This strategy was used in a 'worlds' project and our discussion shows how we took ownership of this idea by naming it.

Bob *In your 'staggered entry' as we now call it they're able to take on lots of all the ideas themselves and develop them into their own stories, so it's a shared development for them, isn't it?*

Judy *Yes. You see there's this problem with the notion of copying and we've got to get over this negative thing about copying. It's learning because if two children are working together and one has got brilliant ideas and the other one has a go at using their brilliant ideas and taking them on board as their own, that's a sort of common knowledge thing as well isn't it? And then the next time this child is in the situation where it needs a few ideas, it's got a springboard, it's learnt a construct, you know, it's learnt what ideas are. It's got a springboard to go from and he or she could*

Framing creativity in your practice: Summary

In this chapter I have been arguing that the identification of a 'bottom up' creative practice in which ownership of that practice is but one consequence, requires the development of frames and amenable and appreciative discourses. This in itself is a creative process. In summary I would like to suggest the following:

* Identifying creative frames in your own practice may be assisted by making use of INSET days, so that teachers and schools may feel that they are maintaining some ownership of their practice.

* Time given to observing and discussing creative teaching in a collaborative   way as described might have the effect of countering the reduced morale (documented by Pollard et al 1994) prevalent in many schools today.

* Since the methods to be used to raise achievement in schools are still under debate, I would suggest that creative practices need to be part of the ongoing conversation over effective pedagogy.

Finally, the nature of a creative practice is more difficult to define than it is to talk about. I hope that the methodological approach which I have described in this chapter assists in discerning that practice particularly in times when alternative, more limited practices based on outcomes models, are more prominent.

References

Bernstein, B. (1977a) 'On the classification and framing of educational knowledge' in *Class, Codes and Control, Vol 3.* London, Routledge and Kegan Paul

Bonnett, M. (1994) *Children's thinking: promoting understanding in the primary school,* London: Cassell

Craft, A. (1991) Thinking Skills And The Whole Curriculum. *The Curriculum Journal* Vol 2,2, Pp 183-199

Craft, A. (1997) 'Identity and Creativity: Educating for post-modernism?' *Journal of Teacher Development,* accepted for publication in May 1997,

Day, C. (1993) Reflection: A Necessary But Not Sufficient Condition For Professional Development. *British Educational Research Journal* Vol 19,1, pp 83-93

Dewey, J. (1929) *The Quest for Certainty: A Study of the Relation of Knowledge and Action,* New York, Minton, Balch.

Eisner, E. (1979) *The Educational Imagination,* London, Collier Macmillan

Fryer, M., Collings, J.A. (1991), 'Teachers' views about creativity', *British Journal of Educational Psychology,* 61, pp207-219

Gates, P (1989) Developing Consciousness and Pedagogical Knowledge Through Mutual Observation in Woods, P. (Ed.) *Working Together for Teacher Development,* Cambridge, Peter Francis

Hargreaves, D.H. (1983) 'The teaching of art and the art of teaching: towards an alternative view of aesthetic learning', in Hammersley. M. and Hargreaves, A. (eds) *Curriculum Practice: some sociological case studies,* Lewes, Falmer Press

Jeffrey, B. (1995) 'Problematising Conversations' Presented at *'St Hilda's At Warwick Ethnography Conference'* Unpublished. Warwick University

Jeffrey, B. and Woods, P. (1996) 'Creating Atmosphere and Tone in Primary Classrooms' in Chawla-Duggan, R. and Pole, C. *Education in the 1990's: Reshaping Primary Education,* London: Falmer

Jeffrey, B. and Woods, P (Forthcoming) *Teaching Under Inspection* London: Falmer

Jeffrey, B. Woods, P (1997), 'in Pollard, A. Thiessen, D. Filer, A., *Children and Their Curriculum: The Perspectives of Primary and Elementary School Children.* London: Falmer

OFSTED (1995) *Guidance on the Inspection of Nursery and Primary Schools.* London HMSO

Pollard, A. Broadfoot, P. Croll, P. Osborne, M. Abbott, D. (1994) *Changing English Primary Schools?*

The impact of the Education Reform Act at Key Stage One. London: Cassell

Schon, D. A. (1983) *The reflective practitioner: how professionals think in action,* Temple Smith

Woods, P. (1990] *Teacher Skills And Strategies,* Lewes, Falmer Press

Woods, P. (1995) *Creative Teachers in Primary Schools,* Buckingham, Open University Press

Woods, P. and Jeffrey, B. (1996) *Teachable Moments: The Art Of Creative Teaching In Primary Schools.* Buckingham, Open University Press

Woods, P. Jeffrey, B. Troman, G. Boyle, M. (Forthcoming) *Restrucuring Primary Schools and Teachers Reconstructions* Buckinham. Open University Press

Woods, P. and Wenham, P. (1995), 'Politics and pedagogy: A case study in appropriation', *Journal of Educational Policy,* 10.2, pp 119-43

Chapter 6

Teaching Style, Culture and Creativity

Anna Craft

All pedagogy is set in a cultural context. Thus notions of what is creativity, and how to foster it, will be culturally defined.

In this chapter I explore some of the connections between culture, pedgagogy and pupil creativity, through the case study of some research which I am collaboratively undertaking with researchers, teachers and pupils in southern Spain.

I begin by introducing the idea of person-centred teaching and learning with reference to a wider literature on teachers and their attributes before looking at how that translates in the Spanish classrooms which form part of the research project. Finally I look briefly at teaching as personal artistry, arguing that it is important for teachers to be able to develop an individual and personal style in the classroom.

Person-centred teaching and learning

Creative teachers are often very 'person orientated' in their attitudes and values. This is well documented by Marilyn Fryer (1996). In her study of 1028 teachers in the UK, she found that the top ten attitudes which distinguished the most orientated to creativity from those least orientated to it, were:

* wishing to deepen learners' understanding of the world
* believing all pupils can be creative
* striving to differentiate teaching for each pupil
* aiming for learners to respond with empathy
* valuing pupil self-expression, and teaching skills which facilitate this

* aiming for pupils to think intuitively
* valuing free expression work by learners
* striving to broaden learners' awareness of the world
* wanting pupils to be able to express their feelings
* valuing pupils' ideas and questions in assessing creativity

(adapted from Fryer, 1996)

Indeed in general, there is evidence, although admittedly pre-National Curriculum, that many teachers of young children enter teaching because of their positive regard for other people, particularly children, over and above their interest in the subjects they are to teach (Book, Byers and Freeman (1983). Person orientation in educators is also a finding in my own research (1996a, 1996b, 1997).

I want to distinguish *person centred teaching* from the set of values which indicate person orientation, because it highlights the people in the learning process above the curriculum. It is similar to the notion of 'unconditional personal regard' which is used in counselling. For me, person-centred teaching and learning does not mean disregarding the curriculum, nor does it mean adopting any one particular teaching style, but rather bearing in mind all of the time that at the heart of any classroom activity is learning, for understanding, which is owned by a learner.

Culture and creativity

Some of my research work is based in southern Spain. During one of my recent visits there a primary teacher expressed the view that creativity had nothing to do with education. What he meant was that in his view, in Spain, teachers and schools are seen as conveying knowledge and skills but not an approach to life which is about creativity. This is a perspective which is held by other teachers with whom I have worked, in both England and Spain. And yet, I have witnessed teachers in both countries facilitating and inspiring creativity in their pupils. But what my work in Spain has made me much more conscious of, is how the surrounding culture affects how teachers do it.

Spain: a case study of creativity in cultural context

Recent reforms in Spanish education brought in the teaching of English to all primary aged children. Teachers are encouraged to draw heavily on social constructivist theories of learning in planning and teaching. Implicit in constructivist theories is the basic idea that the learners make their own sense of any given learning experience and that this is mediated by both the physical and social environment, and the way in which tasks are set up.

The policy then suggests a shift toward greater independence in learners, and potentially supports the demands of post-modern global society. However the culture shift for both teachers and learners is huge, as schools attempt to move away from approaches to teaching and learning which involve less recognition of individuals as makers of sense. It is important to recognise some of the economic and political background to the prevailing culture in schools: some of the factors in this include Spain's economic position as a developing country, and the perceived value of education and of teachers in enabling individual prosperity, also the influence of 40 years of dictatorship followed by 20 years of successful transition to democracy and pluralism.

The implementation of educational reform in Spain has been decentralised so that although there are nationally defined objectives, model materials have also been distributed to schools, in the expectation that schools will produce their own 'curricular project' - or curriculum plans, each year. This is inspected at a regional level, and the inspectorate are not involved in supporting schools in the development of their plans. The models of implementation can be interpreted as threefold, using Chin and Benne's (1970) power-coercive model for the national objectives, their rational-empirical model for the exemplar materials sent to schools, and their normative-reeducative model for the requirement that schools prepare their own curricular project. It has been argued (Shepherd, 1994) that leaving the details of change at the school level places legal obligation on teachers to create change with little experience of how to, because of 'ancien regime' influences on pre-service training in universities, and little tradition of teacher collaboration or team work in planning or teaching. Shepherd argues that the decentralised model of reform, whilst intended to empower teachers and schools, in fact presents a considerable challenge since 'the implementation of the reform 'at the chalk face' has been trusted to those least able, willing or prepared for it' (Shepherd, 1994: 4).

Thus teachers are under more pressure than ever before to foster imagination and creativity, and to teach using social constructivist approaches, whilst being worse prepared than ever before to do so.

To attempt to meet teachers' needs, the Ministry of Education now funds 'grupos de trajo', or working groups, of teachers, which involves a small amount of funding to enable a group of teachers to work together over one or two years on a school-based project. In addition, publishers are working with policy makers and school districts to support change in pedagogy; Shepherd (1994) has argued that published materials can provide an 'open learning programme' for teachers (1994:10). Consequently one of the research team is based at Oxford University Press in Madrid, one of the major publishing houses fostering pedagogic development in the teaching of English in Spain and one aspect of my research there has involved looking at the role of text books in pedagogy.

How we collected our data

With their kind permission, we used an interview based on a questionaire drawing on work by Fryer and Collings (1991). The interviews were conducted in Spanish by teacher training students at Caceres University. Since each student was placed for their teaching practice with the teacher they interviewed, they were also able to observe their practice and note the extent to which their practice bore out their responses to the interview. With another researcher who spoke fluent Spanish I also talked to some of the twenty eight teachers involved in their classrooms and observed their pedagogy.

In general the questionnaire was felt to have been a useful tool and overall, with a few exceptions, a fairly good indicator of pedagogy.

Three features of pedagogy: organisation, discourse, values

The researchers' observations were almost exclusively of whole-class teaching. This in part reflects the dominant local practice. Specialist English teachers work in rotation with different class groups in the school, rather than English being taught by the main class teacher.

We observed a number of general pedagogical features, which we classified for analysis using Robin Alexander's (1996) categories of analysis for whole-class teaching in cross-cultural settings: organisational, discourse and values.

Organisationally, the whole class was almost exclusively taught en bloc, with the exception of some pair role-play in one class, which nevertheless involved the rest of the class watching. There was a level of informality in each of the classes observed, however the teacher remained in charge, usually standing up, mainly at the front of the room, occasionally moving through the rows of children to the other end of the room. In each of the classes observed, the teacher's desk faced the children, and the blackboard formed a focal point on which the teacher wrote frequently during the lesson to illustrate spelling and grammar. Differentiation for children achieving highly or struggling with the lesson content was provided only in terms of the level of spoken interaction with the pupils.

The *discourse* revolved around use of the text book, which in common with local practice, all teachers observed relied heavily upon (one scheme only; no 'pick and mixing'). Each child had a text book open on the desk throughout each lesson even when minimally referred to. The lessons observed involved a great deal of speaking and listening, as might be expected in languages lessons. This was reinforced by the limited wall displays (most classrooms had nothing at all on the walls, and where there were displays they did not include children's (or teachers') work, but rather printed matter, commercial posters and so on. Concepts were taught 'by the book', teachers frequently referring to the manual during the lesson. Understanding was checked by repetition, questioning and through role play exercises dictated by the text book. Pupils appeared motivated even though the content of the learning was not personalised for them. Many children were proud of their language skills and wished to practice with English speaking visitors at the beginning and end of lessons.

Values conveyed by the teachers observed included expectations about behaviour (an understanding that the teacher was in charge) and focus (the learning of each child was the focus). Each child was valued, whilst knowledge manifestly held and passed on by the teacher as expert, backed up by the text book. In the lessons we observed, achievement was defined against the text book criteria of being able to speak, listen, understand and translate key phrases, in an orderly way, following the teacher's guidance. The wider cultural values surrounding the teacher's role, and which were reflected in the lessons we observed, are discussed further later on in the chapter.

Strategies which fostered learner creativity

Strategies associated with particularly effective fostering of pupil creativity included some of Herzberg's hygiene conditions for pupils and teachers, notably involvement in the lesson, intellectually stimulating teaching, monitored student-teacher communication, and structured lessons. These were achieved through:

* use of humour (one teacher used many different techniques within one lesson to get his class laughing, from mixed-up words such as 'dalsa' for salad, 'rtacos' for carrots, to unusual and amusing combinations, such as 'spider steak'),

* friendly coaxing of individuals,

* calling on individuals by name,

* generally high teacher expectations including positive insistence on getting the answers right (for most pupils - not for those who were struggling),

* keeping the pace fast, and;

* using the text book to help structure the lessons.

In such classrooms there was an atmosphere of excitement, of ease and of inclusion. Each child was treated as both a member of the class as a whole, and also an individual in their own right.

Our observations of this group at work have brought out a number of strategies associated with fostering learner creativity within whole-class teaching. Learner creativity in this context meant pupils being able to make connections of their own, to come up with new combinations, to apply imagination to their use of language, to operate as English speakers beyond the particular expectations of the classroom. The strategies which we observed include:

* firm control (teacher-centred but learner-focused)

Control was held in different styles by each individual. In part clearly it came from pupils' expectations, based on previous experience of each teacher. Strategies for holding firm control in a teacher-centred but learner-focused manner included having clear ground rules on classroom management (in general the pupils were all seated, the teacher standing; in general the arrangement of the room meant that pupils and teachers were facing one another, and could easily make eye contact). The pace of the lesson was important; pupils were not given the opportunity to get bored with any concept or activity.

The model of the teacher as source of knowledge was very strong; as was teacher as embodiment of authority. Both of these are perhaps more embedded in Spanish culture than they are in the UK, as I discuss later in the chapter.

Throughout lessons where the teacher was successfully fostering pupil creativity, the teacher remained the centre of control. But at the heart of this was the learner, thus these lessons were 'learner-focused'. Also implied in this term is the powerful use of relationship with individual pupils, discussed next.

* authentic teacher-pupil relationships

Pupils were made to feel that their teacher knew they were there, and that they, personally, mattered. Relationships were authentic; there was a great deal of warmth between teachers and pupils, and a sense in which teachers knew the children's context (for example, their locality), if not the details of their lives. The children's context was a part of the lessons. Thus during a spoken exercise about explaining where they lived, one teacher demonstrated that she knew exactly where each child lived. Consequently pupils were constantly alert for personal contact, focused on their classroom performance. There was a sense in which teachers who were able to foster pupil creativity had 'eyes in the back of their head'.

* use of humour

Humour formed a critical element in these classrooms. It was often unexpected, almost always teacher-centred but pupil focused, and often in English and Spanish, thus woven in with the lesson content. Pace was important; teachers using humour to good effect moved on quickly before the high spirits degenerated.

* high teacher expectations

Making clear to pupils what was expected, by modelling it, was critical. This meant that answers were usually only accepted when they were correct. It was assumed that the vast majority of the class would achieve the same level of expectation during a lesson (although not all did). High expectations were combined with a gentleness and acknowledgement of individuals and their difficulties; sarcasm and irony were not used except in a warm, teasing way.

These strategies mirror the findings of Fryer (1994) who found moderate to high correlation between orientation to creativity and 'person orientation', or the valuing of relationships. She notes that the most creative teachers succeed in actively and deeply engaging each pupil in learning and thinking for themselves. They also echo the recommendations of Shagoury Hubbard (1996) whose writing is based on ethnographic field work in Alaskan primary classrooms. Shagoury Hubbard talks about pupil creativity being fostered in an environment which has both structure and freedom; flexible predictability, where pupils are respected as capable thinkers, where expectations are high, and where relationships between adults and children are authentic.

The playfulness involved in using humour is documented by Gardner (1993) and also Shagoury Hubbard (1996) as a critical part of fostering creativity.

Summing up themes and initial findings in the Spanish project:

General themes, then, which have emerged in the Spanish teachers' contextual attitudes to imagination and creativity, and in the translation of these into practice, are:

* social/caring orientation of this group; valuing thinking about others, being affectionate and emphasising learner characteristics which are about self-esteem, relationship, confidence and communication

* hard-working response to the job: the majority of teachers in this group feel they work very hard and are very busy. This may well reflect the demands of the job and also the gender balance of the sample (mainly women with family responsibilities also).

* positive outlook of the group

* an approach to creativity which includes seeing connections, involving divergent thinking, awareness of beauty, as inspiration and as connected with aesthetic value.

* strong views that creativity in education is not just about ideas, that it is not about some school subjects only, and that it can be crafted

* placing of high value on classroom control in the classroom, getting learners involved, and strong pupil-teacher communication.

Comparisons, carried out by teacher training students, of observations of the teachers at work with their stated attitudes, indicated that there are sometimes gaps between teachers' stated attitudes and their practice, although this was unusual rather than the norm.

Pedagogic style and pupil creativity

One of the issues which interests us in this research project, is the connection between pedagogic style and teachers' capacity to foster pupil creativity, in the sense of the children being able to create new possibilities in the English language, both in speaking the language and in using it as a tool to create ideas and combinations novel to the learner. The vast majority of work observed so far has, as indicated, involved whole-class teaching - reflecting the dominant pedagogy locally.

The research team's own observations of this group at work have brought out so far a number of strategies associated with fostering learner creativity within whole-class teaching. These include (as explained above):

* firm control (teacher-centred but learner-focused)

* authentic teacher-pupil relationships

* use of humour

* high teacher expectations

There is some evidence from other studies (Fryer, 1989, 1993, Fryer and Collings 1991) that gender is an important factor in pedagogical approach; women tending to adopt a 'pupil-oriented' approach (believing that anyone can be creative and that creativity can be developed), and men adopting an 'instrumental' approach (concern with mastery of basic skills, achievement of high academic standards and behavioural expectations). Fryer (1996) also suggests that teachers of languages and arts are much more likely to adopt a pupil-orientated approach, and those teaching maths, science and technology are much more likely to adopt an instrumental approach. We have not yet found this in the Spanish project. Indeed, what we have observed about pedagogy, involves a combination of both approaches, within the teaching of English, and the teacher's gender does not appear to be a factor in the balance of approach taken.

The pedagogical strategies described above include a strong element of teacher as 'mentor' to the class, in being more skilled in the language, and helping individuals come to their own understandings and develop their own skills in it. Interestingly, Shagoury Hubbard (1996), Fryer (1996) and Torrance (1984) have all recommended the key role of teachers and/or other adults as mentor (on a one-to-one basis) in supporting the development and expression of pupils' creativity. Shagoury Hubbard also talks about children taking on the mentor role where appropriate - although we have not observed this happening in the Spanish classrooms.

Cultural relevance of 'creativity' in the Spanish context

As indicated earlier, it is important to acknowledge the place within society of both teachers and creativity. In the Spain, all teachers are civil servants, with permanent posts. Teachers are viewed as authority figures within the community and accorded respect by pupils and parents. Schools are considered to be places of professional expertise. Deference is shown toward the teacher's professional judgement - even when, as was the case with one teacher observed, the teacher in fact knows little about the subject being taught (this particular individual had been allocated the teaching of English because he had studied French as an undergraduate, and was the only member of staff who had studied languages to degree level; however he was unable to hold a conversation in English and took advantage of having two English speaking visitors in his classroom to learn from native speakers himself, alongside his class).

Consequently teachers in Spain have a strong sense of professional purpose and to a degree consider themselves expert in their domain. As discussed earlier, if this is undermined it is done so from within the education system (through teachers' perceptions of the reforms in education), rather than from outside.

However, during informal discussions with students and with the research team, few of the teachers in this sample considered creativity to be particularly relevant to society. This pattern of values may reflect the economic and social context in Spain, where the impact of the accelarating pace of global technological and social change is not felt in any real way yet. It may also reflect the stability felt by teachers as authority figures embedded in their communities.

The lack of importance accorded to creativity in education has been documented elsewhere. From her research with teachers across the UK, Fryer (1996) describes how only 17% of teachers in the Collings and Fryer survey (1991) were really positive about creativity.

It seems likely however, as argued by others (Helgesen, 1990, Egan, 1992, Glasser, 1992) that the pace of global change will demand an increasing emphasis on fostering pupil creativity. In my view this will involve using pedagogy which involves both person centredness and intentional strategies, perhaps in the ways described in this chapter. What is important however is that pedagogy should belong to the culture of which it is a part. So, pedagogical styles which are appropriate in Southern Spain may not be so in Madrid, or in London, or Glasgow, or Llandridod Wells. And this also means that what counts as pupil creativity is influenced by the cultural and domain context.

Teaching as personal artistry

In his studies of the creativity of primary teachers, Woods (1990, 1995) and Woods and Jeffrey (1996) have described many different pedagogic styles and strategies undertaken by creative teachers of primary aged children. One of the strongest themes in their work is of just how individualised each teacher's art is (for they do describe teaching as artistry). As Woods and Jeffrey (1996) put it, 'There are biographical, situational, institutional, structural, resource and relational factors that go into the social production of creative thinking' (p2). They emphasise the roles of intuition and instinctual judgement in the art of teaching, and describe the complex skills involved in the balancing of different priorites, dilemmas, pressures, demands, which teaching involves, as *orchestration*. This is a metaphor which I love, as it conjures the image for me of a diverse but organic whole, which through the insightful leadership and direction of the conductor, becomes much more than the sum of its parts. Bob Jeffrey's exploration of 'frames of creativity' in Chapter 2, exemplifies his approach to exploring teaching as artistry. For Woods and Jeffrey (1996), as for others such as Jackson (1992) and Hargreaves (1994) what is key is 'the emotional heart of teaching' (1996: p4). They acknowledge the personal desire and individuality within the role.

I find the notion of teaching as artistry a far more appropriate model than others (such as teacher as technocrat, or as manager) which have become dominant in recent years in many parts of the world and commented upon by others such as Cocklin, Retallick and Coombe (1996). And just as culture clearly forms an important part of the backdrop to creative teaching, a key principle which seems to me important in being able to facilitate learner creativity is to have adequate space to develop one's own personal artistry. Clearly, culture is likely to have some bearing on how far teachers perceive this need for personal artistry: certainly the Spanish teachers in our research study did not state a need for personal expression of their professionalism, however English teachers in a different study I have recently undertaken, did (Craft, 1996). Nevertheless, no two teachers in the Spanish study taught in an identical fashion, and the pedagogy of each did have a strong personal flavour. In Chapter 7, I look with Tom Lyons at some suggestions for exploring and developing one's own artistry.

Summary of Chapter 6:

In this chapter I have introduced the notion of teaching as 'person centred', as a background to my exploration of the pedagogy of teachers in southern Spain. I have introduced the project, its methodology and the educational reform context. Using Alexander's (1996) analytical categories I explored the Spanish teachers' pedagogy in terms of:

* organisation,
* values, and
* discourse.

I have identified features of pedagogy present in classrooms where learner creativity seemed to be being fostered; these included

* use of humour,
* friendly coaxing,
* calling on individuals by name,
* high teacher expectations,
* fast pace, and
* structured lessons (often using text books)

Aspects of the cultural context in which these teachers worked included whole class teaching, high value placed on the text book and high respect accorded to the teacher as a community figure. Pupil creativity was characterised in terms of competence as speakers of English. I have described several intentional classroom strategies for fostering learner creativity within whole-class teaching. Overall the Spanish teachers demonstrated strong person-centred attitudes to teaching, and I have summarised some of the key aspects of their attitudes to creativity. Significantly, the notion of 'creativity' having any relevance to what teachers do in schools was considered tenuous by many of the teachers in the project, reflecting, I would suggest, wider social values.

Finally I have related the cultural saturation of teaching to the notion of teaching as artistry, since culture to some extent influences the extent to which teachers value personal expression in their professional role.

Acknowledgements

I would like to thank in particular the teachers and students who have participated in the study to date. Thanks also Toni Pain at the University of Caceres, and Rick Shepherd at Oxford University Press in Madrid for their support and collegiality in designing and undertaking our collaborative research project investigating pedagogy and creativity, which began in early 1996 and which I have referred to in this chapter.

References

Alexander, R. (1996), *Other Primary Schools and Ours: Hazards of International Comparisons,* CREPE Occasional Paper, The University of Warwick: Centre for Research in Elementary and Primary Education

Book, C., Byers, J., Freeman, D. (1983), 'Student expectations and teacher education traditions with which we cannot live', *Journal of Teacher Education,* 34, p 30-51

Chin, R. and Benne, K. (1970), 'General strategies for effecting change in human systems', in Bennis, W., Benne, K. and Chin, R. (eds), *The Planning of Change,* London; Holt, Rinehart and Winston

Cocklin, B., Coombe, K., Retallick, J. (1996), Learning Communities in Education: Directions for Professional Development, Paper presented at the *British Educational Research Association Conference,* Lancaster, 12-15 September, 1996

Craft, A. (1996a), 'Nourishing Educator Creativity: A Holistic Approach to CPD, *British Journal of Inservice Education,* Vol. 22, No. 3, Autumn 1996

Craft, A. with Shepherd, R., Pain, T. (1996b) Creativity and Pedagogy in Spain, Working Paper September 1996

Craft, A., (1997), 'Nourishing Educator Creativity: A Holistic Approach to CPD, *British Journal of Inservice Education,* Vol. 22, No. 3, Autumn 1996 [in press]

Egan, K. (1992), *Imagination in Teaching and Learning,* Routledge, London

Fryer, M. (1989) *Teachers' Views on Creativity,* Unpublished PhD thesis, Leeds Metropolitan University, Leeds

Fryer, M. (1993), 'Facilitators of Creativity'. Paper given at the 39th Creative Problem Solving Institute of the Creative Education Foundation, Buffalo, NY

Fryer, M. (1994), 'Management style and views about creativity', in H. Geschka, S. Moger, and T. Rickards (eds) *Creativity and Innovation: The Power of Synergy,* Geschka & Partner Unternehmensberatung, Darmstadt, Germany

Fryer, M. (1996), *Creative Teaching and Learning,* London: Paul Chapman Publishing Inc

Fryer, M., Collings, J.A. (1991), 'Teachers' views about creativity', *British Journal of Educational Psychology,* 61, pp207-219

Gardner, H. (1993), *Creating Minds: An Anatomy of Creativity Seen Through the Lives of Freud, Einstein, Picasso, Stravinsky, Eliot, Graham and Gandhi,* New York: HarperCollins Inc

Glasser, W. (1992), *The Quality School,* Harper Perennial, New York, NY

Hargreaves, A. (1994), *Changing Teachers, Changing Times: teachers' work in the postmodern age,* London: Cassell

Hegelson, S. (1990), *The Female Advantage: Women's Ways of Leadership,* Doubleday, New York, NY

Jackson, P.W. (1992), *Untaught Lessons,* New York: Teachers' College Press

Shagoury Hubbard, R. (1996), *Workshop of the Possible: Nurturing Children's Creative Development,* Maine: Stenhouse Publishers

Shepherd, R. (1994), *Educating for the Future: A case study in change implementation at national level,* unpublished submission for part of MA in Applied English Linguistics (Option: Managing Change), University of Birmingham, 1994

Torrance, E. P. (1984) *Mentor Relationships: How they Aid Creative Achievement, Endure, Change and Die,* Bearly, Buffalo, NY

Woods, P. (1990), *Teacher Skills and Strategies,* Basingstoke: The Falmer Press

Woods, P (1995), *Creative Teachers in Primary Schools,* Buckingham: The Open University Press

Woods, P. and Jeffrey, R. (1996), *Teachable Moments,* Buckingham: Open University Press

Chapter 7

Nourishing the educator: knowing what you need

Anna Craft and Tom Lyons

In this chapter we draw on our research project (1995-6), which focused on how the educator can be nourished as a facilitator of creativity in children, and what educators may need to sustain their vision.

The chapter moves from an introduction to the idea of knowing and nourishing oneself, to examining what we have discovered about what nourishes the educator. We explore three principles for nourishment: risking being more than what you teach, openness, and letting your unconscious out.

In the final part of the chapter, we make some suggestions about self esteem and allowing ourselves to be seen. We finish with some practical strategies for educators to use, for self-nourishment.

Introduction: knowing and nourishing oneself

One of the biggest challenges for teachers is knowing oneself. In developing strategies for matters such as mentoring, or fostering creativity, however, we often forget to think about ourselves as teacher, *our* needs and wants.

Teachers, particularly of young children, traditionally have a strong social/caring orientation (Acker, 1995, Woods, 1990, 1993, 1995; Woods and Jeffrey, 1996; Pollard, 1987, 1989, Nias, 1989). They are often very hard working and very busy (Fryer and Collings, 1991, Craft, 1996a). However as Heather-Jane Robertson's work suggests, discussed by Craft (1996b), this could reflect gender and/or the demands of the job (or a mixture of demands, such as the job plus other family resonsibilities) just as much as personal characteristics.

The feeling of 'being there' for the children, of the work never being complete, of one's own needs as irrelevant except insofar as they directly impact meeting the perceived needs of the children, is very common and manifests itself as feelings of guilt (Hargreaves and Tucker, 1991).

Knowing oneself is not easy. It means acknowledging feelings in professional life and development. It potentially allows professional self-study to have an impact on self-esteem. As Marian Dadds (1993, 1995) puts it, 'studying our professional work may mean studying aspects of our daily life which run close to our hearts... the more attached we are to our work... the more likely it may be that our feelings will be closely implicated'. Teachers involved in our recent study (Craft, 1996b) said they felt that knowing oneself was extremely challenging, since their role as a teacher was to provide, and they had tended to think of their own needs as irrelevant.

Drawing on our research project with educators in the South-East of England, we would argue that knowing and nourishing oneself as an educator in any domain is critical to being able to provide for others. This is because genuine relationship, with oneself and with others, is at the heart of the process of creativity.

Evidence: background to our research project

During 1995/6, we carried out a small research project with eighteen educators in the South-East of England. The group had all enrolled on a postgraduate course on *Creativity in Education,* taught at The Institute for Creativity and assessed by The Open University. The course was innovative and experimental, offering a holistic approach to continuing professional development. It combined experiential work with study and practice-based project work, and involved emotional and spiritual support as well as academic analysis.

The educators who studied the course included five youth workers, eight school teachers (across the primary and secondary sectors) or further education lecturers, one governor trainer, two LEA advisory staff, one facilitator working with adults in creative personal development and one designer working with interactive educational multi-media materials.

In collecting our data, we used a range of methods, including participant observation of the course, tape recording each session. We also used questionnaires and formal, transcribed interviews.

Further details of our project can be found in a seminar paper (Craft and Lyons, 1996) available from Anna Craft at The Open University, and also in two journal papers (Craft, 1996a and 1997), also in an article written for *The Times Educational Supplement* by Jonathan Croall (1996).

What nourishes the educator?

During our research project we discovered a number of themes which the educators held to be important. Where we found four or more educators making the same point, we classified this as a theme. The more educators making the same point, the stronger the theme.

An underpinning belief of the group was that **for the educator to be creative, s/he needs to be nourished**. For the educators in our project, nourishment included taking time for personal development. They had a positive attitude toward their own personal nourishment and were much less focused on the practical questions of legitimation (within the curriculum structure), resourcing (time, materials, equipment, energy), support (colleagues, critical agent, critical others, receptive pupil culture). In contrast, Peter Woods has documented these as being very important to teachers whom he worked with (1995). The educators in our project, began instead from a position of belief in 'creativity as a good thing' regardless of these contextual issues.

But as indicated in the introduction, taking time for personal nourishment doesn't come easily to teachers as a group. Hard-working, caring, conscientious and self-effacing in many ways, teachers as a profession tend to put the needs of learners in front of their own wants. In our research group, there was a theme of

personal and/or professional change having moved individuals to take this particular course. For many (ten - ie over half) of the group they had reached some kind of crossroads, or had experienced some kind of 'critical incident' which had influenced their choice to undertake the course and to emphasise their study of creativity. Sometimes, critical incidents can be a powerful way of making a change. Here is how one educator put their decision to enrol on the course:

'I suppose because of all the stuff that's going on for me at work and personally at the moment I am very aware of the feelings of getting squashed that happen when you don't get the support... you don't get the recognition.... you don't get the enabling that you want from a particular route.....' so I ... thought to myself ... let's go for it'

Another teacher put it like this:

'The course has come ... at a particular rather vibrant period of my life and I am in the process of change ... last year I made the sort of bold step to actually claim some of the creativity I knew I ought to be working on by doing a big play [at school] and that taught me quite a lot... that plus a personal situation has opened up how I see my immediate future'

For several other teachers the bad experience of OFSTED had motivated them to enrol on the creativity course, as a basis for re-focusing their professional artistry. We use the word artistry as it was used in chapter 6, to emphasise their experience of contrast between the complex *craft* of teaching, and the professional identity which goes with that, compared with their experience of OFSTED (which seemed to de-professionalise their work to much more of a technician-type approach).

Of course, the decision to nourish yourself doesn't only result from experiencing some kind of critical incident. But it is probably something which you need to choose consciously, so that you can monitor the extent to which you are succeeding! The act of choosing is a key part of being creative, as Robert Fritz says (1946).

Being motivated to find ways of nourishing yourself

may be a mixture of personal and professional, or they may be more one than another. One teacher told us that she needed to do lots of her own activities (such as hat-making and dress-making) in her spare time, as that provided a source of inspiration for her. Another decided she wished to travel, so cleared a short space so that she could do so. Another realised he didn't take enough exercise in the countryside any more, and committed to having a long walk at least once a week with his partner. Professional examples of nourishment included a teacher in a management position wanting to develop her creativity by getting some kind of peer supervision and feedback, also a primary teacher wanting to feel some 'ownership' over his job after an OFSTED inspection, rather than feeling controlled and pressured from statutory bodies outside of the school.

Within our project, some of the things which nourished the teachers were emotional support, being part of a student network, getting feedback on their skills and general personal presentation (written and oral) away from but linked with their normal teaching and learning situation, the challenge of studying at MA level. Some of the teachers worked in the same school. Most of the teachers in that group got a great deal from studying and developing together, although one said they would have preferred a bit more distance.

So, what nourishes the educator is very personal. There are many other forms of nourishment than studying for an experiential-based MA level course, too. For some people, working in a conducive environment is key. Or it may be your out-of-school activities which nourish you; a sport perhaps, or going to hear live music, travelling, or going to the theatre, or seeing friends and family, or reading, or .... the list is endless.

What is important is that you choose it.

Choosing a creative path

We take the view that creativity is dispositional and not a matter of ability. In other words that choosing a creative path in any given situation is less a matter of ability to do so and more about 'mind-set' or attitude.

Being creative means being inclined to be, and being sensitive to opportunities in which to be so. This is a perspective adopted by David Perkins and colleagues at Project Zero at Harvard University (Perkins, Jay and Tishman, 1993). They argue that *ability* to be creative is the third aspect of being creative, but that the *habit* of being inclined to creative behaviour and the *quality of alertness, or sensitivity,* to opportunities for creative behaviour are just as important.

As Robert Fritz (1946) says, being in the creative orientation means being willing to make choices, and to break the tension between the 'now' and 'possibility'. As an example, one teacher we worked with, felt that getting feedback from her colleagues was very important indeed as a source of nourishment. So although she felt a bit shy of doing it, she suggested setting up a peer-mentoring system with one colleague in particular. They called it a 'critical friendship'. In telling us about it she said:

'We have tried it before but this term we have made it more formal and divide the time between ourselves and we have a kind of informal contract to both give encouragement but also to challenge each other... that really fascinates me as a process because it's very creative'.

And making choices can feel like, or actually involve, taking a risk. Through risk comes change, and change is at the core of growth and development.

Risking being more than what you teach

A useful question to ask yourself is the one often asked by Jana Dugal, Director of the Institute for Creativity: 'Am I what I teach?' Most teachers have a very strong identity as a teacher, particularly those teaching 3 - 11 year olds. However, do you allow yourself to be swallowed up by teaching, and what you teach? Asking yourself the question, 'Am I what I teach?' on a regular basis, is a way of starting to identify what you need in order to be 'you'. And being more aware of the nourishment which you need for yourself is a critical part of being able to foster creativity in others.

The commitment to 'risk' - another strong theme in our research project - provides another practical challenge. 'Risk' implies a broaching of boundaries, the 'going beyond', the breaking with convention described by Gardner (1993a). Examples from our project ranged from a teacher of six and seven year olds adapting his plans at the drop of a hat to take his class outside into the snow even though it was not encouraged within the school, and a youth worker deciding to create a workshop on acappella (unaccompanied) singing for young women only, where they could compose and perform songs from the heart (which resulted in discovering that one child was being abused; it also resulted in another child gaining enough confidence to go for a recording contract with a record label, which she achieved). It seems likely, as Hargreaves has predicted (1994), that we will see an increasing recognition by educators of the need to take risks, for themselves and for learners with whom they work.

Finding out what you need is a process which can bring with it surprises! It can also mean taking some risks. Risking hearing things which you didn't know you were seeking, and which you may not know how to accommodate.

Openness

The belief that creativity involves 'receptivity' or 'openness' to a wide range of influences, including spiritual and intuitive ones, was a theme which emerged from our research project. It echoes points made by Fritz (1943) about having vision and then allowing ideas to 'germinate' and 'assimilate', and by Gardner (1993b) about valuing creativity across the different intelligences. It also echoes the writing of Cziksentmihalyi (1994) in which he reports that artists with whom he worked demonstrated openness to experiences and impulses, and Gardner's (1993a) discussion of great creators.

Personal nourishment involves the same quality of openness, or receptivity. One educator in the project awoke in the middle of the night feeling a burning sensation in her mind and body. She found herself first writing it as a poem and then painting it.

Eventually this process provided the focus for a workshop which she offered at national conference. It is similar to the experience reported earlier in chapter 2, of the educator who awoke in the night hearing music playing, and who played it out on the piano, eventually making it in to a learning experience in her educator role. The act of being open both nourished her unconscious self, and was also integral to both of these educators' roles in fostering creativity with learners. Another teacher described how at the time in his life when he got married, he was somehow able to be receptive to lots of impulses and ideas which in his conscious mind he didn't know were there - leading to a huge class-based project with the infant children he was teaching. The act of being open, which originated in his personal life, nourished his unconsious self in enabling a new idea to grow and be implemented in school. And a teacher of drama described great enjoyment of expressing her own feelings to her students, and vice-versa.

Letting your unconscious out!

One of the primary teachers in our project told us 'I don't think you can separate yourself and your teaching'. And a powerful part of yourself is your unconscious mind, the source of impulses, sensations and feelings, and which is often non-logical. When we talk about nourishing your unconscious, we are referring to Assagioli's (1974) distinction between the '*I*' and '*self*', the former referring to sensation, emotion/feeling, impulse/desire, imagination, thought, intuition, and will. The 'I' refers to the conscious self which has the capacity to transcend, or disidentify from, the 'self'.

What follows are five practical strategies for letting your unconscious out. We have named them as follows: looking at your 'reflection'; giving yourself space; remembering your dreams; imaging/ visualisation and finally, making images concrete.

i) Looking at your 'reflection'

In our project we noted the tendency to **value aspects of creative teaching which they themselves want/ need.** 'Mirroring' in this way is widespread in personal growth literature (Edwards, 1993). Other traditions, such as the psychoanalytic, call it 'projection' - Freud first described it as a 'defensive mechanism' operating in the cases of hysteria which he was studying (1894). Later, he called the same defence mechanism 'repression', and later still his daughter Anna Freud (1936), listed projection as just one of twelve aspects of repression. The idea was later developed by Melanie Klein (Segal, 1964, Ogden, 1982). The idea in projection is that sometimes people feel and behave as though important aspects of their own selves are contained in others.

You can turn these ideas around, by noticing:

*....how you organise your life at present: everything which you do serves a purpose for you, even if it doesn't feel like it! Some of your current way of living already nourishes you as a creative educator. This is like looking in the mirror, to see what is already there!

*....what you tend to have a strong reaction to in your life. There may be situations or people who really make you frustrated, and others which you adore. Often we are more aware of what annoys us than what makes us happy. And what annoys us is often a reflection of something within ourselves which we dislike, or which needs attention.

A part of the creativity in education course involved a weekend workshop, entitled *The Mastery,* taught at The Institute for Creativity. Focused on creating and performing in front of an audience, and giving and receiving feedback, it is in many ways structured around the process of looking at one's own reflection. Many teachers in our project commented on the depth and power of that experience; words which were used included 'magic', 'absolutely mind-blowing', 'changed my life, so they say'. Most echoed the comments that *The Mastery* 'gives you permission to explore roles and facets of yourself', and that 'it made you re-examine (your practice)... you know we are all sitting there being stopped by what we think is circumstance but is mostly ourselves, and we ought to get on and do these things really'.

That creativity requires ownership and relevance has

been well documented (Woods, 1995, Woods and Jeffrey, 1996). 'Looking in the mirror', or looking at your 'reflection' helps you to see what resources and activities you already have at your fingertips, and perhaps some of the challenges. And, of course, although *The Mastery* is a process which can enable you in doing this it is by no means the only, or 'the right' way to do so; it is important that you find a way which is appropriate for you.

(ii) Giving yourself space

The notion of clearing time and space was embedded in the course which our research group participated in. It has also been acknowledged by other researchers, such as David Feldman (1994), who has written about the way in which the non-conscious mind synthesises ideas and information in a way which can appear to be co-incidental to our conscious selves. He argues that insight comes from listening to messages which our non-conscious selves are sending us - through, for example our dreams and daydreams. What is important is that we may get flashes of information about a particular aspect of our lives over and over again during a long period of time. If we are to make use of and act on them, we need to make space and time to listen to them.

Space and time may be as short as ten minutes. But finding space regularly is what matters. Space may be also physical; it may involve being in a quiet place, or walking, or swimming, or being in a place of worship, or sitting with a cup of tea, or even meditating! What is important is that the space should be empty, and without expectations. It is just time for you, to re-charge and to hear what your spirit might need as nourishment. Julia Cameron (1995) calls this 'making a date with yourself'.

Some people find it really useful to write things down. If you choose to do writing in your personal space, remember that the main point is to allow the ideas to flow, rather than censoring any. So think in terms of just writing, say for two or three pages, without judgement, just as you would if you were brainstorming, except that you may choose to write prose. Some people call this process 'journal writing'.

For examples of how this can be done, see Holly (1989).

Clearing a space in this way can provide you with direct nourishment or even inspiration. Or it may simply clear a space, for you to be in better contact with yourself.

(iii) Remembering your dreams

As David Feldman (1994) has argued, new visions, ideas and projects often come to us in symbolic form. Our dreams can be a powerful source of information, and also inspiration. Writing down your dreams can shed light on how your unconscious might like to be nourished. Get in to the habit of jotting down (notes are enough) what you can remember of your dreams, first thing each morning, or whenever you can manage it.

One of the authors has a strong recollection of a dream she had shortly after taking on her first leadership role in education. She was involved in a spinning game (holding hands and spinning round and round, as children do) with the previous leader, and they were surrounded by the team who sat watching in a circle. Her sense was that the centrifugal force would eventually lead to one of them letting go, and that whoever let go first was the 'loser'. She awoke before the dream ended, but the lasting impression was of the feeling of rivalry, and of her discomfort. She realised that to feel nourished in this role, she needed to complete the relationship and the baggage from the previous leader, which she then set about doing. In fact this led to a different leadership structure. Although the context was a youth club, and the author was sixteen at the time, the principle of remembering and interpreting dreams, especially powerful ones, is just as relevant to her today, and in any context.

Dreams can hold very simple messages, in symbolic form. They can be interpreted in many ways. What is really important, is what they mean to you. They can hold within them the solutions to puzzles we have been wondering about, as well as inspiration and vision. And they belong to us; it is just that we are not always in tune with this abundant and often wise part of ourself!

(iv) Imaging/visualisation

As Jung discovered (1995), the symbolic forms of dreams can be a part of waking life too. Visualising, or imaging, are easy-to-use techniques which enable us to draw on the metaphors which our unconscious constructs. Imaging, or visualisation, involves relaxing into a semi-meditative state, and then allowing images to form in your mind's eye. You can image or visualise along a specific theme or question, such as 'relationships' or 'what shall I do for assembly', or 'the impending OFSTED inspection', etc. Since what you conjure up comes from your own unconscious wisdom, you can also ask questions of it.

One of the authors was recently trying to decide which path to begin to take at work: more administration, or more research. Having relaxed deeply, she visualised a symbol of each option. The symbol for the administrative work turned out to be a stiff, outdoor broom, tidily and briskly brushing up everything in sight. The symbol for the research turned out to be a beautiful, deep red and gold flower, very soft and inviting. The broom was too busy to hear the questions she was posing, whilst the flower asked questions in return. The combination of the feelings conjured up by each image, and the stimulation offered by the one image and lack of it conjured by the other, helped her to make the decision to alter her career course for a while.

A classroom teacher whom one of us knows, tried visualising when her relationship with the head teacher got rather strained. In her visualisation, the symbol for the headteacher was a bush. It was blocking the path, but she saw that the path was surrounded by rough scrub which although not neatly laid out like the path, was quite easy to walk on. She decided to walk around the bush, without being blocked by it. As she did so, she saw that the bush, although large, was in fact quite spindly. As she walked around it, it seemed less important and powerful than it had previously. She drew on her visualisation in taking the decision to work as closely as she could with the deputy and to distance herself from the head - thus 'going around' the head.

Several of the educators in our study visualised themselves as a tree, growing in a nurturing environment, for the duration of the course. They interrogated their visual images, to find out what kinds of nourishment would be most appropriate for the tree (ie for themselves).

For very practical guidance on how to use visualisation and image work, see Edwards, (1993), Gawain, (1978), Glouberman, (1989). All three offer different ways of inviting and then working with images.

(v) Making images concrete

Try sculpting, painting, drawing, playing, writing or even acting out your images. The therapeutic traditions have a long history in making concrete the unconscious in this way. Making your images concrete, in much the way of brainstorming, can be enormous fun as well as actually help your decision making.

Self-esteem and vision

All of the practical strategies involve ways of nurturing self-esteem. A powerful theme in our own research was the belief that self-esteem and self-confidence must be nourished in order to be creative. This applied to educators as well as to learners. Concern with esteem reflects the social and caring orientation of our particular research group, who in this respect were typical of educators as others have documented (Collings, 1978, Fryer and Collings, 1991, Acker, 1995, Hargreaves and Tucker, 1991, Hargreaves 1994).

Working with others

Many teachers in the project told us that they needed personal autonomy, and to feel comfortable with their own **'artistry'** as an educator (the idea of artistry is explored in several of the chapters in this book including chapters 2, 5, 6 and 9). The teachers in our project expressed the need to feel able to be 'themselves' as professionals, rather than playing a role ascribed to them by others' expectations. One teacher even described the feeling of exposure and vulnerability which he experienced when unable to have professional autonomy as being 'akin to the removal of trousers'.

What may underly this expressed need for 'autonomy' in the teaching situation is that the scope it gives the impusive, creative 'me' to surface more readily, without the judgement/social control of the 'I'.

But working with others is a key aspect of teaching, whether you are teaching in a one to one situation or in a school with classes of up to 35. Relating, and relationship, with colleagues and with children, are central to all that happens in a teaching and learning situation.

'Relationship' was a major theme emerging from our project: in other words almost all of the educators involved in it said they valued highly the notion of **'relationship'**. This was not defined solely in terms of teacher/pupil; teaching and learning were characterised as *roles* which could be undertaken, and thus the learner sometimes became the teacher and vice-versa. Many referred to creativity as 'being in relationship', meaning that dynamic interaction, with oneself or others or both, as essential to creativity. Several talked of empathising with learners. One said 'it's about responding to where they are at and I think that can be quite creative... you pitch in as to where they are coming from, you automatically click into a game of understanding... you are trying to stand in their shoes all the time basically'... and another said 'I think it is sometimes just picking up what has meaning for the children'. Talking of how she might approach sex education with her own daughter, one educator said, 'I would find a way of finding out where she is at so that I can communicate with her on that level. Now for me that's being pretty creative'.

Others commented on how different aspects of their lives felt fragmented, and how bringing these parts together through 'self-acknowledgement', felt essential to creative action with others - 'becoming a connected person' as one participant said, 'rather than being disjointed and unconnected which is what a lot of us walk around being'. A youth worker expressed it like this: 'In people I work with [I aim to] develop their uniqueness and their emotion, although I try to do that all the time, I think I could do that better if I know myself more...' An LEA advisor described his need to bring together his home and work selves: 'it's actually getting in touch with your own creativity and the roots of it and the sources of it and trying to work it in, in a vocational sense, into one's job... the creative part of me and the work part of me, they are doing this... (gestures that they are travelling separate routes and are disconnected). These comments demonstrate the Assagiolian notion of the transcendent self bringing together aspects of the unconscious self.

'Being in relationship' also extended to interaction with all constituencies involved in fostering creative action (ie other colleagues, learners, parents, other agencies). For example a governor trainer said: ''I need to... make people aware... and not just the teachers and not just the governors and not just the children but the parents, that as a partnership ... [all of those] agencies ... are involved in the education of the person...'

'Relationship' as a component of creativity, extended, too, to the need for audience. This was sometimes expressed at the level of what they themselves needed in order to be creative; one person recognised their own need for an audience - and another felt that what was created was in dynamic relationship with the creator: 'the creating and the created have consciousness and being about each other so there is relationship [and audience] right from the minute the impulse begins'. Another felt that 'you yourself have a relationship with the subject [you are teaching], ...so you bring energy in with you.... creativity is shaping energy... I think we associate creativity with the idea of bringing a lot of yourself to it'

Most educators also commented on the quality of the teacher/learner relationship. Several educators commented on the need for a good relationship with learners 'before you start anything too experimental... So that ... they know where your borders are before you start' (infant teacher). Many said how much they enjoyed being 'in relationship' with learners, as this comment from an FE lecturer shows: 'I think what

nourishes me is.... the students, I am nourished by students' feedback', and this comment from a primary teacher: 'I think the kids keep me going to be honest... I enjoy it, I enjoy being with the kids, they give me a buzz' - and from this infant teacher: 'the children are the inspiration'..

Implicit in all of the references to 'relationship' was this sentiment expressed by one of the group: 'through the right kind of relationships that teachers have with people, they will liberate the creativity that their students have'.

'Being in relationship' can also be threatening. One educator said, 'I am not into personal relationships, but that is so important in education'. Reflecting on how he had come into education, he went on to say: 'you don't necessarily go into education for the relationships quality you go in for the subject element and therefore that's one of the reasons why we hit all the problems in secondary education'.

The emphasis on 'relationship' in our research group reflects the focus and findings of much literature researching teachers' work (Woods, 1990, Woods, 1995, Woods and Jeffrey, 1996, Cooper and McIntyre, 1996a, 1996b). The importance of 'relationship' to learners is also well-documented, both in terms of relationships beteween learners and in their relationships with educators (Cullingford, 1991, Delamont and Galton, 1987, Jackson, 1987, Pollard, 1987, Sluckin, 1987).

Knowing what you need for yourself, in order to function happily and willingly as a part of dynamic relationships with colleagues and pupils, is really vital. We hope that the practical strategies suggested in this chapter may help you to identify your own needs.

Summary of Chapter 7 so far:

Drawing on our research project we have suggested that:

* one of the biggest challenges for teachers in knowing and nourishing oneself, and that
* choosing the creative path in your life and in your practice is dispositional and not a matter of ability.

We have proposed a number of practical strategies to enable you to become more than what you teach, which include fostering greater openness and letting your unconscious have greater agency, including:

* noticing your 'reflection',
* giving yourself space,
* remembering your dreams,
* imaging/visualisation,
* making images concrete.

Finally we have explored aspects of self esteem embedded in some of these practical suggestions, in order to foster your professional artistry.

The final part of this chapter is about becoming 'visible' in your creativity and in ensuring you get the nourishment you need in order to enable creativity in others.

Being seen

This chapter has been about 'being seen', initially by yourself. It has been based on the principle that our unconscious can offer us access to all kinds of inspiration, and often knows what the next steps in any project may be. And that knowing yourself includes having some access to your unconscious mind! The practical suggestions on how to develop your access to your unconscious are based on the idea of 'composting', or 'mulching'. It isn't that your plasticine model of last night's dream will get translated directly into story time with your reception class, just as one rotten apple in your compost heap won't translate instantly into new fertiliser for the rose

bush. But allowing your unconscious out in many different ways will, over time, combine together to provide a rich ground for inspirations and choices to take root and grow.

Filling in the blanks: a series of snapshots

The last part of this chapter is a blank space, for you to jot down initial thoughts on what nourishment you need. As our needs change over time, think of this as just one step in a process; a snapshot of where you are today!

Nourishment I would like as of today (Date:)

Acknowledgements

We would like to thank all of the educators with whom we have worked, and whose practice has informed this chapter. Also Jana Dugal and Christine Kimberley at The Institute for Creativity in London, with whom so much of our own thinking and research on creativity has developed, through the collaborative presentation of our innovative postgraduate MA level course 'Creativity in Education', which The Open University accredits. Thanks also to Professor David Perkins at Harvard University whose discussion of creativity as dispositional with one of the authors was invaluable. Finally, thanks are also due to our colleagues in the Centre for Curriculum and Teaching Studies at The Open University, who have awarded grants to support some of the research.

Bibliography

Acker, S. (1995), 'Carry on Caring: the work of women teachers', *British Journal of Sociology of Education,* Vol. 16, No. 1, 1995, pp 21 - 36

Assagioli, R. (1974) *The Act of Will,* London: Wildwood House

Cameron, J. (1995), *The Artist's Way: A Spiritual Path to Higher Creativity,* London: Pan Books

Collings, J. A. (1978) *A psychological study of female specialists in the sixth form,* Unpublished PhD thesis, University of Bradford

Cooper, P and McIntyre, D (1996a), *Effective Teaching and Learning: Teachers' and Pupils Perspectives,* Buckingham: Open University Press

Cooper, P. and McIntyre, D. (1996b), 'The importance of power sharing in classroom learning', in Hughes, M (ed), *Teaching and Learning in Changing Times,* pp 88-108, Oxford: Blackwell

Craft, A. (1996a), 'Nourishing Educator Creativity: A Holistic Approach to CPD, *British Journal of Inservice Education,* Vol. 22, No. 3, Autumn 1996 [in press]

Craft, A. (1996b), *Continuing Professional Development: A Practical Guide for Teachers and Schools,* London: Routledge

Craft, A. (1997), 'Identity and Creativity: Educating teachers for post-modernism?' in the *Journal of Teacher Development,* May 1995 [in press]

Craft, A., Lyons, T. (1996), *Nourishing the Educator,* (Seminar paper 1 of the Creativity in Education Seminar Network) - available from Anna Craft at The Open University.

Croall, J. (1996), 'Time to explore the hidden depths of your own creativity', *The Times Educational Supplement,* 5th April 1996

Cullingford, C. (1991), *The Inner World of the School,* London: Cassell Educational Ltd

Cziksentmihalyi, M. (1994), 'The Domain of Creativity', in Feldman, D. H., Csikszentmihalyi, M., Gardner, H. (1994), *Changing the World: A framework for the study of creativity,* Westport, CT, Praeger Publishers

Dadds, M. (1993), 'The Feeling of Thinking in Professional Self-Study', *Educational Action Research,* Vol. 1, No. 2

Dadds, M. (1995) 'Continuing Professional Development: Nurturing the Expert Within', *Cambridge Institute of Education Newsletter,* No. 30: Autumn/Winter, 1995

Delamont, S., Galton, M. (1987), 'Anxieties and Anticipations - Pupils' Views of Transfer to Secondary School', in Pollard, A. (1987), *Children and Their Primary Schools,* London: Falmer Press

Edwards, G. (1993), *Stepping into the Magic,* London: Piatkus

Feldman, D. H. (1994), 'Creativity: Dreams, Insights and Transformations', in Feldman, D. H., Csikszentmihalyi, M., Gardner, H. (1994), *Changing the World: A framework for the study of creativity,* Westport, CT, Praeger Publishers

Freud, S. (1894), *The Neuro-Psychoses of Defence (1): Standard Edition of the Complete Psychological Works of Sigmund Freud,* Vol. 3, London: Hogarth Press and the Institute of Psychoanalysis

Freud, A. (1936), *The Ego and the Mechanisms of Defence,* London: Hogarth Press

Fritz, R., (1943), *The Path of Least Resistance,* Salem, MA, Stillpoint

Fryer, M., Collings, J.A. (1991), 'Teachers' views about creativity', *British Journal of Educational Psychology,* 61, pp207-219

Gawain, S. (1978), *Creative Visualization,* San Rafael, CA: New World Library

Gardner, H. (1993a), *Creating Minds: An Anatomy of Creativity Seen Through the Lives of Freud, Einstein, Picasso, Stravinsky, Eliot, Graham and Gandhi,* New York: HarperCollins Inc

Gardner, H. (1993b), *Multiple Intelligences: the theory in practice,* New York: HarperCollins Inc.

Glouberman, D. (1989), *Life Choices and Life Changes Through Imagework: The Art of Developing Personal Vision,* London: Unwin Hyman

Hargreaves, A., Tucker, E. (1991), 'Teaching and Guilt: exploring the feelings of teaching, *Teaching and Teacher Education,* Vol 7, No 5/6. pp 491-505, London: Pergamon Press plc

Hargreaves, A. (1994), *Changing Teachers, Changing Times: teachers' work in the postmodern age,*

London: Cassell

Holly, M. L. (1989), *Writing to Grow: Keeping a personal-professional journal,* Portsmouth, NH: Heinemann

Jackson, M. (1987), 'Making Sense of School', in Pollard, A. (ed), *Children and their primary schools,* London: Falmer Press

Jung, C. J. (1995), *Memories, Dreams and Reflections,* (Recorded and edited by Aniela Jaffe, translated from the German by Richard and Clara Winston) London: Fontana Press (originally published in German under the title of *Erinnerungen, Tauma, Gedanken,* copyright held by Random House Inc. 1961)

Nias, J. (1989), *Primary Teachers Talking,* London: Routledge & Kegan Paul

Ogden, T. H. (1982), *Projective Identification and Psychotherapeutic Technique,* New York: Jason Aronson

Perkins, D., Jay, E., Tishman, S. (1993), 'Beyond Abilities: A Dispositional Theory of Thinking, *Merril-Palmer Quarterly,* January 1993, Vol 39, No. 1, pp 1 - 21, Detroit, Michigahn: Wayne State University Press, USA

Pollard, A. (1987), 'Goodies, Jokers and gangs', in Pollard, A. (1987), *Children and their primary schools,* London: Falmer Press

Pollard, A. (1990), *Learning in Primary Schools,* London: Cassell

Segal, H. (1964), *Introduction to the Work of Melanie Klein,* London: Heinemann

Sluckin, A. (1987), 'The Culture of the Primary School Playground, in Pollard, A. (ed), 1987), *Children and their primary schools,* London: Falmer

Woods, P. (1990), *Teacher Skills and Strategies,* Basingstoke: The Falmer Press

Woods, P. (1993) *Critical Events in Teaching and Learning,* London: Falmer Press

Woods, P (1995), *Creative Teachers in Primary Schools,* Buckingham: The Open University Press

Woods, P. and Jeffrey, R. (1996), *Teachable Moments,* Buckingham: Open University Press

Part 4

Vision

Introduction

Vision is a rather under-used term in education. Given the massive and far-reaching changes in global society and the pace of change, together with the past record of education systems in providing a focus for the development of social and economic structures, it seems odd that vision is not a part of the conversation in schools, LEAs and in the wider political process.

Instead, the discourse focuses on issues of a different order, which include standards of achievement, discipline, school attendance, and so on. The need to address each of these issues and many others is not in dispute. What seems odd to me, however, is that the broader conversation is absent. The broader conversation would to my mind include questions about the nature of the school curriculum, its relationship with learning throughout life, and of teaching and learning processes which might support young people's capability in designing their lives with confidence. Such 'life-design' skills include the capability to both recognise and enter into new domains as appropriate. The coming of the new millenium brings into sharp focus these and other questions, as we try to imagine what education could look like in ten or fifty years' time. The two chapters in Part Four of this book bring a practical approach to constructing vision.

Chapter 8, Systems Design for Education, by Gordon Dyer and myself, asks how schools can co-create vision within education and proposes a framework and process for so doing. The chapter is intended to have direct practical application in helping teachers and schools develop their broad intentions for supporting children's learning. It draws on 'systems thinking' which takes account of different parts of the organic whole developing and implementing vision in co-operation.

Chapter 9, written with Jana Dugal, addresses some barriers and challenges to vision in education, by exploring beliefs. We look at blocks to both individual creativity and vision, as well as some wider systems issues which can challenge vision. It, too, is a practical chapter. In it we suggest a range of processes and strategies for facilitating vision, which are intended for use by either individuals or groups.

I hope that this final part of the book will prove practical for teachers and schools, and will thus help foster new millenium vision which education greatly needs.

Anna Craft

Chapter 8

Systems design for education

Gordon Dyer with Anna Craft

In this chapter we introduce a practical, systems-based approach to collaboratively designing educational vision within the school community. The approach which we describe draws on 'systems thinking' and thus acknowledges that school development is organic and complex.

Introduction

The aim of this chapter is to introduce some emerging concepts and practice of social systems design. These were initiated by Bela Banathy (1991), based in California, where he is Senior Research Director in educational research and development and also Emeritus Professor of Systems Science. The ideas involved in social systems design are being carried forward by a world-wide team of researchers who are part of the International Systems Institute (ISI). A major focus for this team is 'systems design for education'. Details of ISI can be found in Appendix 3 at the back of the book.

The traditional approach of systems practice

"Systems thinking and practice" has been used to help with organisational and other management problems (which display complexity and interconnectedness) for nearly 50 years. Take a common problem in primary classrooms: children queuing for their turn on the computer/s. A typical systems approach (eg Checkland,1981), would begin by analysing the situation in terms of " a human activity system" with inputs and outputs, and try to explain its behaviour in terms of interconnected components and processes. This would show exactly how, when and why queues occur, and what objectives were not met.

Next, a new system might be conceived which could be seen as "feasible and desirable to improve in some way". This system would have a clearly specified boundary and objective.

For example, in the case of the primary school problem described above, one traditional systems response would be to aim for a system which increases access for all children to computer based-activity and which is self regulating, so that queues are no greater than 10 mins for any one child. A range of change strategies which might contribute to these objectives would be considered. These might include timetabling: making the computer available during assembly, story time, even break times. Other strategies might include increasing the size of groups of children working on the computer from pairs to, say, four at a time - and perhaps investing in a computer projection screen to enable many more children access to the learning associated with the computer. The idea is that all and any of these strategies might be incorporated in new arrangements, in a new system, so that the queues are reduced to the level specified. In effect, a 'fix' has been put in place.

But this traditional systems approach does not help when there is an almost infinite variety of perceived problems, such as occurs within social systems; boundaries are difficult to draw and issues of power blocking change seem overwhelming. Quite simply, 'fixes' do not work!

A new approach: 'systems design'

Systems design has introduced a new approach to major issues of this kind and, indeed, to the prospect of the future. Its proponents argue that instead of accepting the declines in society which most identify, and to be powerless in facing further decline, communities should take steps to design and create their own future. The approach involves the development by a designing community at whatever level - be it family, small social unit, school, club, association, local community, national community, global community - of a new vision of what they require, an Ideal vision (as described by Ackoff, 1981), which then defines a goal towards which that community collectively and purposefully designs its journey. This approach involves co-designing with others and with the environment. The ability to perform this kind of co-creativity demands a leap out of the current situation and frameworks for education, and for a new interpretation of the requirements for systems for human learning and development which should be designed for the future.

This approach to the future calls itself systems design, as it retains key characteristics of systems or holistic thinking. Thinking systemically, we should harness everyone's creative ability and not just that of the elite. In systems terms it makes no sense to waste resource potential and that is exactly what we do when design is carried out by a few on behalf of the rest. Yet this is exactly the outcome arising from some aspects of our existing education system, in which some people fail to meet achievement targets. Such people often end up being excluded from design decisions affecting their life and their future. In contrast, systems thinking explicitly requires empowerment of, and participation by, all those who are affected by design decisions. Systems thinking enables all individuals to actively participate in their own life-design.

The approach is called systems design, because design in the most general sense, is purposeful creative action; the building of relationships between people and their world. As Banathy (1994) defines it:

"Design in the context of societal systems such as education, is a decision-oriented, disciplined inquiry. People who serve the system and are served by it collectively create or recreate a system based on their expectations and aspirations in co-ordination with their environment."

A culture change is required to bring about the kind of transformation that systems designers argue is needed. In the next part of this chapter, we make the case for a re-visioning of what education is for, as distinct from revising or reforming it - and for a learning and human development system which is based on a very different set of assumptions to the ones we currently use. From this we explore how to develop a vision, and we then go on to look at what

this means for learning arrangements, and finally at the work of the International Systems Institute (ISI), as a mentor in systems design for education.

Summary so far:

We have introduced the notion of systems thinking and practice as an approach used to think about complex issues involving much interconnectiveness. We illustrated some of the principles of traditional systems thinking, ie that problems and their solutions involve:

* inputs and outputs
* clearly specified boundaries
* clearly articulated objectives within the boundaries
* specified strategies for achieving the objectives.

We described the traditional systems approach as being about 'putting a fix in place'.

We then went on to describe a new approach which is emerging within systems thinking: 'systems design'. This approach is modelled on an organic model of envisioning the prospect of the future. It involves:

* the development of a new vision by collective action by communities (such as social units, clubs, schools, associations, etc);

* each individual member co-designing, or co-creating, with others - in this way participating actively in their own life-design;

* harnessing everyone's creative ability and not just that of the elite; and

* building relationships between people and their world.

We have suggested that a culture change is required to bring about this new model of design. In the next part of the chapter we look at what systems design might involve for education. We start by looking at how change in education can be characterised at present.

The Case for Re-visioning Systems of Learning and Human Development

Here are three stories, to introduce the case for a complete transformation of the current education system into revisioned systems of learning and human development which are needed for the 21st century and beyond. The clients for this design are those yet unborn— the children of the 21st century... so in his seminars on this topic, Gordon invariably sets aside a chair ... an empty chair ... to remind participants of this.

Story 1... has a science fiction setting. An alien from Alpha Centauri 3 was sent to Earth to report on what he found. Exploration of this kind took the form finding out how the local species invested their effort. The alien discovered that the 3 top industries on earth .. as measured by turn-over and other economic data are: oil production, weapons production and coffee production.

He sent back his report. "I find Earthlings a very strange breed .. they spend most of their time spoiling the planet's surface while they excavate a strange black substance; their next favourite occupation is killing each other ..while they drink coffee. I suggest we leave this undeveloped place alone for at least 3,000 Earth years." (Collen 1996)

Story 2... came from a discussion at a meeting of the International Society of General Systems Research some years ago. A group of systems thinkers were discussing how it could be?, why it was?, that some people on Earth over-produced food and then wasted it, and others starved. The debate was very animated, and someone else attracted by the noise came into the room asked what going on . "Oh", someone said, "we are discussing the problems of world starvation." "Oh, I see" said the visitor, "I am only a biologist. That's nothing to do with me". He turned on his heels and left.

Story 3... comes from Peter Checkland, well known in the systems field who relates how he became a systems practitioner /management consultant after starting as a chemist. Having taken 3 years of his life to complete his PhD, he said to his supervisor, "After all that effort, how many people do you think will read my dissertation?".

Long pause and obvious thought... then... "Do you mean world-wide?".
Checkland feeling pleased and quite important by that question....
"Oh, yes". Long pause... "About, ...five".

These parables are meant to demonstrate that typically the purpose of education and any debate about re-emphasising purpose is linked primarily to economic considerations or to the self-serving nature of the existing education structures and establishment. It does not take place in a societal context of social needs..

Yet education is continually being changed or reformed. Typically this involves:
- doing more of something
- doing the same but doing it 'better'
- doing the same but doing it 'better' for less
- then restructuring which is apparently called for.

But everything about education remains in its box ... it's based on an old image... the classroom at the centre, and education as a factory with outputs. We use old methods to fix it... by asking questions like:

- what is wrong with the system?
- how can we improve it?, restructure it?
- how can we provide more teaching time?
- how can we decrease class size so pupils get more teacher attention?
- how can we improve behaviour?
- how can we improve pupil, teacher and school performance?
- how can we get more support from our school governors?
- how can we increase achievement in mathematics so that pupils' achievements compare favourably with those of children in Pacific Rim countries?
- how can we increase achievement in reading?
- how can we increase achievement in the sciences and technology so we as a nation can compete

better in the economic arena?

These are all important questions. The point is, that the current approach to change in education (from policy makers and government as well as from within the professional education community) is based on a systems-analysis approach, which is inadequate, because it assumes a cause-effect relationship between education and wider society. This relationship is in reality far more complex. Society includes, and influences, education: the way we conceive of, organise, and 'do' it.

Another weakness in the current approach to change in education is that it asks no questions about the form of education system, in relation to the challenges and realities present in society, at any level. Reform has so far accepted the current forms of provision for pupils aged 3 - 13, ie playgroups, pre-schools and schools. And the current forms of provision may not be the most appropriate ones for the political, social, economic and spiritual transience which characterises the end of the twentieth century. Changing demographic structures and patterns of work mean that more and more parents are lone, and income-earning, meaning that fewer children have care facilities available to them at home. Consequently the need for the care of young children is ever increasing, whilst the demands on their education are much more open-ended than they have ever been before.

Re-visioning education

Questions such as those in the list above are no longer the appropriate ones to base our design for education system for the 21st century because they constrain potential solutions, by defining too narrowly the question. We must seek to understand the issues in a broad societal context — which means a set of complex, interconnected and interdependent problems. The main context is that we have moved from the Industrial Age to the Post-Industrial Information/Knowledge Age. This in turn has created massive changes, massive discontinuities and transformations in all aspects of our lives; requiring changes and transformations in the way we think about education, the way we perceive the social function of education, and the way we provide arrangements for learning and human development. Recent changes in education fail to recognise the development gap.

Questions with greater relevance might be:

- What is the nature and what are the characteristics of the emerging post-industrial information/knowledge age?

- What are the educational implications of those characteristics?

- What framework can we use to re-think education and what vision, core ideas and core values might inspire our thinking?

Fig. 3 provides a possible interpretation of the first question, adapted from Banathy (1991), which provides a contrast of some of the general features.

So then we need to ask ourselves about the educational implications of the characteristics of the information/knowledge age.

Organisations and management thinkers have already recognised the impact of the rapidly changing environment. We can detect shifts in what is being suggested as the paradigm for the desirable characteristics of organisations, i.e they are to become open, dynamic, flexible, to be functional and evolutionary, to enable empowerment to capture everyone's potential creativity, they are to be learning organisations which learn from failure rather than place blame, in which people cooperate and act supportively, and seemingly emphasise quality rather than quantity.

If we accept this is a valid statement, then there is a distinct conflict between these needs and the current education system which is designed to produce failure, ranking and to engender competition. In short there is a mismatch here. It is a miracle in a sense how young people make the transition between what they learn from their school experience and what they are expected to do within the so-called learning organisation. For many young people, if they succeed it may be despite the education they experience. So,

Fig. 3

	INDUSTRIAL/ MACHINE AGE	INFORMATION/ KNOWLEDGE AGE
KEY CHARACTERISTIC	extension of physical powers by machine technology	extension of cognitive powers by cybernetics/systems technology
PROCESS ORGANISATION	around energy for machine technology	around intellectual technology for information/knowledge development
PARADIGM	Newtonian classical science; deterministic; reductionist; single causality; organized simplicity	cybernetics/systems science emergence; multiple causality; dynamic complexity; ecological orientation; concern for non-renewable resources
TECHNOLOGIES	inventing, fabricating, manufacturing, heating, engineering	gathering/organizing/storing information; communicating, networking; systems planning/designing
PRINCIPAL COMMODITIES	energy, raw and processed materials, machines, manufactured goods	theoretical knowledge and information to support policy formulation, systems design, human services
ECONOMY FOCUSES	on high volume production	on high-value production
SOCIAL CONSCIOUSNESS	is based on national and racial identity	extends into global consciousness

drawing on the third question above, there is a need for a new vision within education.

Transcendence, Re-visioning and Transformation.

The fundamental approach to systems design is based on the 3 stages of Transcendence, Re-visioning and Transformation. It can be illustrated by the following questions:

Q1. What kind of society would you like to see for your children and your grandchildren?

Q.2. If we have such a vision, what kind of learning agenda and education system would serve that society?

Q.3. If we are serious about nurturing human potential and serious about the learner as client - and not the teacher, can we project a system of learning arrangements and resourcing, and opportunities for learning, that are relevant to the learner and which will enable such a vision?

Q.4. What is the methodology by which we design such a system?

The questions are iterative - in other words, they follow on continuously in a spiral of development: having got to the end of the questions, you begin again at the first one.

The first question involves transcending - getting above all of the nitty gritty day to day constraints and opportunities of educating, and looking down on the entire system in a conceptual 'bird's eye view'. It is easy to allow current realities to constrain our visions of what may be possible. But that is the very point of a vision. It transcends what we currently have and know. It's a bit like a very big 'brainstorm', something which primary teachers often do with children, and used to do when planning learning.

The following questions (about the kind of learning and form of education which might serve the society and enable the vision, and the methodology by which we might design such a system) are focused on re-visioning and transforming.

Developing a Vision - getting practical

In the rest of this chapter, we look at how a vision can be developed in practice - for example, in your school. If you are interested in following up the principles of Systems thinking, you might like to investigate some of Bela Banathy's books, listed in the references.

Systems design argues that in order for a community to co-create they must first collectively develop a vision. Time and extensive consultation within a community is needed to do this. Communities will need to acquire the skills to undertake the process.

One of the authors has designed a starting draft (Dyer, 1995) which has been demonstrated as adaptable for use in a range of small social units, which could include an educative unit for children aged 3 - 13. He has named it 'a Family declaration of interdependence'(Fig. 4). An example of how it can be applied follows. The idea is that the statement of ideals will continue to evolve.

The idea of the family declaration is that the small social unit, such as the school (and preferably all staff, non-teaching included) images its own 'Ideal', and then uses the declaration above as starter in starting to make the vision concrete. Though written as a declaration for staff, we believe that children should be encouraged to participate in the development of the declaration.

The declaration of interdependence immediately begs the question, what rights does each individual have, and what responsibilities? So the next step is to debate and create a 'Bill of Rights and Responsibilities'. It is by agreeing on who has a right to what, and how individuals are responsible, that the 'Declaration' gets embedded into practice, and starts to get 'owned' by all of the people it concerns. A draft bill might look something like that shown in Appendix 1.

If you would like to have a go at drafting your own Declaration and Bill of Rights and Responsibilities, turn to Appendix 2.

The process which Gordon Dyer (1995) has developed for re-visioning involves four stages, as follows:

Introduction (involves establishing Ideals, drafting Declaration of Inter-dependence, sharing views and amending the draft) - and this stage can involve as few as two people

Development(involves cascading dialogue with others, amending the draft, and collectively clarifying it)

Incorporation (involves developing a Bill of Rights and Responsibilities)

Review (involves reviewing the experience of the Family or team, so far, and amending the Declaration and the Bill). The process then runs through again, and again, and again, and so on. (See Fig. 5)

The XYZ School Staff Group Declaration of Interdependence - a Statement of Ideals which will continue to evolve

We the members of the XYZ School Staff Group
who share interest and care for one another and for the education and development of the communities in which we live, do hereby declare and pledge to honour our interdependence.

DECLARATION OF COMPASSION

Equality begins here, with me.
I, as one of the Staff Group, will treat everybody else in the Group in the way I would like to be treated. I will actively practice compassion with everyone, including those who are not like me. I will seek, first, to understand, then to be understood.

DECLARATION OF DIVERSITY

We are as one.
Our diversity serves the School, the local Community and the Nation. We learn from each other. We need and encourage diversity. We support, and are supported by, each other. Our strength and power comes from our differences. I will respect
each person's right to be different from me, whether or not I understand or like the difference. I will not discriminate against members of the Staff Group because their ideas, beliefs, and behaviours are different from mine.

DECLARATION OF DEVELOPMENT

Change begins with me.
I will respect each individual and support his or her development. We will delight in the prospect of new members joining us and we will work to incorporate their views in this Statement of Ideals. I will take responsibility for the shaping of the culture within the Staff Group.

I will make a conscious effort to encourage positive, constructive growth in the Group. I will support an environment which is free of hostility. I will make a conscious effort to intervene in behaviour that I find inappropriate by supporting open communication and by establishing common goals and common ground.

DECLARATION OF EXCELLENCE

We strive for excellence
I am proud of the contributions that all of us make to the Staff Group and to my own community. The Group and I are valuable assets to the community.

I realise that I will not always be able to live up to this Declaration of Interdependence. However, all of us, working together through mutual inquiry and conversation, can contribute to make the Group better, now and in the future, and to make a significant contribution to the larger community.

Fig. 5: systems design cycle

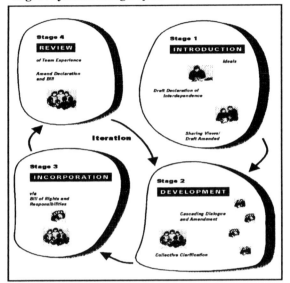

SYSTEMS DESIGN METHODOLOGY WITHIN A TEAM

Interdependence is key to all that we have explored in social systems design, so we look next at what this means for arrangements for learning.

Translating interdependence into learning arrangements

Interdependence is a large concept and it will be important for any community to develop and clarify their own interpretation of it. Key within interdependence will be rights and responsibilities. A key issue will be, how do we develop individuals and communities so that can accept their rights and responsibilities in a framework whereby everyone recognise their interdependence to set alongside their independence? Primary schools traditionally involve a great deal of independent working and learning. For teachers - often working in relative isolation from one another for much of the day, and for children - often studying, in practice, on their own rather than collaboratively or as part of a grouping (Galton et al, 1980a, 1980b, 1992, Webb, 1993), or talking at low-level (Bennett et al 1984) - such as who should have the unifix cubes. Development work such as that by Wragg, Bennett and their colleagues at Exeter University, on how to develop truly collaborative group work needs to become part of primary practice

.(Dunne and Bennett, 1990, Bennett and Carre, 1993, Wragg, 1993a, 1993b, Wragg and Brown, 1993, Brown and Wragg, 1993, Wragg and Dunne 1994).

Summary so far:

We have suggested that there are weaknesses in the current approaches to change in education. Questions about the form of educational system in relation to current challenges and realities in society are not being asked. We suggested that the search for potential solutions is constrained by too narrowly defining the question.

In contrast we introduced the notion of re-visioning education, which involves acknowledging the social and economic context of our questions, ie the Post-Industrial, Information or Knowledge Age. We provided a brief contrast of this with the previous, Industrial Age. The kinds of questions which might be posed in contemporary social and economic life are consequently, we suggested, much broader, and take account of the nature of the age in which we live, and consequently the forms of education which might be appropriate within it. We proposed the three fundamental stages in systems design:

* transcendence,
* re-visioning, and
* transformation.

We illustrated some of the practicalities of developing a vision through these stages, through a process designed by Gordon Dyer (Appendix 2). An evolving process, involving a continuous cycle of four stages:

* introduction (establishing ideals, and a declaration of interdependence which outlines the vision)
* development (cascading, debating, amending, the vision)
* incorporation (Bill of Rights and Responsibilities)
* review (reviewing and evaluating, amending and beginning the cycle again)

To help make the process more tangible we provided an example of what a bill of rights and responsibilities might look like.

Similarly work on transforming the community of schools to become co-creative, is already under way through work such as David Clark's (1996).

And of course between the ages of 3 - 13, children develop through childhood, puberty and maturity. There is an expectation within the individual, the community and society, that each young person becomes more and more independent. It is possible to envisage dependence and independence as opposite ends of a spectrum or dimension, where at a given time individuals will be experiencing a position based on their particular stage in their growth and development as an animal (physical dimension), and on a variety of other dimensions related to their development as an active, thinking, caring member of a particular community, or position in relation to defined constructs within their society. So whereas children entering reception class may be relatively independent at the physical level of being able to eat with a knife and fork, go to the toilet independently, tie shoelaces and do buttons, they may be relatively dependent on the spectra of being able to write or read unaided. And of course the extent to which individual children are dependent or independent will be an individual matter; for example some children cannot do buttons when they enter Reception, and others can already read independently.

The arena of social constructs is the most complex in that it will contain many spectra along which dependence and independence can be interpreted. The position achieved on any spectrum will depend on the power (in terms of position, resource, expertise and personal power) that the individual has developed within a range of social constructs and which are valued within that culture. At any given time an individual will be dependent to a particular degree, for example, on the social welfare system, the educational system and on an organisation for paid employment. In the typical Western culture and in the organisational forms which are common, to be independent is usually regarded as a strength. Conversely, to present as dependent is often seen as a weakness. The degree to which this generalisation will apply depends on the cultural and organisational

context. But for example, most nurseries and primary schools have an entry-level assessment process which specifies the extent of independence in young children in being able to hold conversations, concentrate, do physical tasks, etc. This is repeated at the start of most school years, and at transfer between schools, for example from infant to junior, from first to middle. The nursery and National Curriculum assessment systems require such assessments, and the process is, along with teaching and learning, inspected by OFSTED.

There is then, a strong sense in which the education system which supports these social constructs, accepts competition as inevitable and relates its provision to these values and constructs. We may characterise the learning agenda of the current education system as being tailored to a culture of the development of independence as an Ideal.

We can represent it like this:

dependence ——————> independence

In stark contrast, one strong message arising from the future Ideal which drives systems design of education is that to some degree we are all dependent on each other - we are interdependent - the young should themselves be better prepared to take part in the process of defining that interdependence. For relationships to be effective, individuals must have both the psychological and material independence in order to enter effective communication with others. It requires an education for the individual by which they will be encouraged to firstly understand themselves and to be allowed to develop fully as individuals. Their education should also develop in them the values and skills of systems design conversation and dialogue, of creating an atmosphere of mutual tolerance, and of recognising interdependence and the value of diversity. It should encourage co-designing and team-work. In short, an aim of systems design of education must be to bring about an adaptation from its basic culture of the development of independence in individuals as Ideal, to a culture where development of independence takes place alongside the development of values and skills sponsoring human interdependence, as co-Ideals. Agreeing the balance between these co-Ideals and setting the parameters of the design journey towards their achievement will be the prerogative of each community.

We fully recognise that collaborative and team work is a natural part of some schools' approach to teaching and learning. Some examples of co-creative, inter-dependent learning are: designing classroom 'ground rules' at the start of a school year; paired reading; imaginative play; mini-enterprises or simulations; circle time (such as those developed by Murray White, 1991, 1992, 1994a, 1994b, 1995).

The Fifth Literacy

The requirement to develop such co-creative skills will apply as much to adults as it will with the young. It adds a new dimension to the phrase "learning society", which it is argued must now include the development of systems design skills, as well as coping with new technologies and development of personal IT skills which are currently seen as the main drivers for a learning society. Such skills have been called the Fifth "Literacy" (Banathy, 1992 and 1996) to add alongside the original 3 R's, and Computer literacy. Developing our co-creative skills includes having better access to our intuition and unconscious, and communicating with others at that level. Jana Dugal calls this 'communicating through your essence' (1996).

In the final part of the chapter we look at what systems design in education might lead to!

Mentoring systems design for education

Through the process we have described so far, in due course children and young people will have some opportunity to learn through actual experience of systems design being practised in the social units in which they are members. But given the expected long term timescale for dissemination we need to consider what learning arrangements within society might be appropriate to facilitate the re-visioned systems of learning and human development; in other words how

---

Summary of learning and the fifth literacy:

We have suggested that any community group will need to develop and clarify their own interpretation of interdependence, as it might apply to learning arrangements. We have proposed that some of the elements to consider (and which indeed some schools are already working to) might be:

*   the ways in which teachers themselves work,

*   the extent to which collaborative practice is or should be part of children's learning,

*   expectations which might change over age,

*   cultural assumptions about the role of independence' in contrast with 'interdependence',

*   ways in which future learning systems might embrace both the education of the individual and also the interdependence involved.

We proposed that the need to develop co-creative, inter-dependency skills may form a 'fifth literacy', which along with the 'three R's and computer literacy, and are important for adults as well as for children.

---

the vision might be 'mentored'. The example below presents a contrast between the existing system of education and a possible future system of human development and learning.

It is a very controversial image of course, as it makes no assumptions about the continued existence of schools, colleges and universities as we know them, or the governance systems which we currently have. The image which follows is typical of that which members of the ISI would support. More about this organisation and its role as a mentor in systems design for education can be found in Appendix 3.

THE IMAGE OF THE EXISTING SYSTEM	THE IMAGE OF A DESIRED FUTURE SYSTEM
Education is an instrument of cultural and knowledge transmission, focusing on maintaining the existing state and operating in a rather closed system mode	Education should reflect and interpret the society as well as shape the society through co-evolutionary interactions, as a future-creating, innovative and open system
Education is an autonomous social agency separated from other societal systems	Education should be coordinated with other social and human service systems, interpreting learning and human development
Education now provides instruction to individuals during their schooling years	Education should provide resources, arrangements, and life-long experiences for the full development of all individuals and the society
Education focuses on the basics and preparation for citizenship and employment	Education should cover the coexistence of many domains, including the sociocultural, ethical, moral, economic, physical/mental/spiritual, scientific/technological and aesthetic
Education is now organized around the instructional level : arrangements are made that enable teachers to present subject matter to students	Education should be organized around the learning-experience level: arrangements should be made in the environment of the learner by which to master the learning task
Today teacher-class and teacher-student interactions are the primary means of the educational experience	We should use a variety of learning types: self-directed, other-directed, individually supported group learning, cooperative learning, social and organizational learning
The use of educational resources and arrangements is very much confined within the school , colleges and universities	We should use the large reservoir of learning resources and arrangements within society

Conclusions

To transcend and re-vision the current education system implies that we can first form a vision of the society we require and then the system of education, or better defined as "system of learning and development" which would serve that society. The suggested way ahead is to develop within communities the competence to create their own future... their Ideal and for them to chart their pathway, or navigate towards that Ideal (Horiuchi 1994). This requires the development of a design competence at all levels - families, small social groups, local communities, wider communities. The International Systems Institute is working to develop a body of knowledge and practise which will help educators and communities in this task. In parallel with this endeavour, it is argued that another aim of systems design of education is to bring about some adaption from its basic culture of the development of independence in individuals as the Ideal, to a culture where development of independence takes place alongside the development of values and skills sponsoring human interdependence, as co-Ideals. So the challenge for future systems of human development and learning must include developing the capacity in individuals and groups to- transcend, envision, and transform... and that this should be seen as the fifth great literacy to add alongside the 3 R's, and computer literacy. This is our focus for creativity - co-creativity. To do this will demand that we acknowledge the truth of Christine Kimberley's moving words at the 1996 Creativity in Education Conference, held at The Open University in London (Kimberley, 1996):

"The only resources we have at our disposal when we enter this world are the Earth's physical resources and our imagination"

Summary so far:

If you think Seasons   *grow crops*
If you think Decades   *plant trees*
If you think Centuries   *educate your children*
                    (Ancient Chinese Proverb)

In this chapter we have outlined the views of the proponents of systems design of education. We have put forward the view that the transition to a post-industrial/information/knowledge age (or even the age of Consciousness as described by Andrew Billen in *The Observer*, September 1996), which is accompanied by massive social discontinuities, means that we should not simply extend education into the 21st Century, we should transcend it; we should not simply revise education, we should re-vision it; we should not reform education we should transform it. Notwithstanding the apparent difficulties and the long term nature of this approach we must start out now on this design journey, for if we do nothing about the future, then the future takes care of itself... that is not a nice prospect given further declines which are in prospect.

References

Ackoff, R.L. (1981), *Creating the Corporate Future*, New York: Wiley

Banathy, B.H. (1991), *Systems Design of Education; A Journey to Create the Future*, Englewood Cliffs, New Jersey, USA

Banathy, B. H. (1992), 'Systems Design: The Third Culture', *Educational Technology*, August 1992, New Jersey: Englewood Cliffs

Banathy, B.H. (1994), 'The Three Imperatives of Systems Design of Education: Transcend - Envision - Transform', *Educational Horizons*, pp 186-193, The National Honor and Professional Association in Education, Bloomington, Indiana

Banathy, B.H. (1996), *Designing Social Systems in a Changing World*, New York: Plenum

Bennett, S.N., Carre, C. (1993), *Learning to Teach*, London: Routledge

Bennett, N., Desforges, C., Cockburn, A., Wilkinson, B. (1984), *The Quality of Pupil Learning Experiences*, London: Lawrence Erlbaum Associates Ltd

Billen, A. (1996), 'The New Age Gurus', *The Observer*, Sunday 1st September, 1996

Brown, G. and Wragg, E. C. (1993), *Questioning*, London: Routledge

Checkland, P (1981), *Systems Thinking: Systems Practice*, Wiley, New York

Clark, D. (1996), *Schools as Learning Communities: Transforming Education*, London: Cassell

Collen, A (1996), A conversation with Gordon Dyer at Fuschl, Austria, April 1996

Department of Education and Employment (1996), *Nursery Education Scheme: The Next Steps*, London: HMSO

Dunne, E. and Bennett, S.N. (1990), *Talking and Learning in Groups*, London: Routledge

Dugal, J. (1996a), 'Communicating through your essence', unpublished presentation, September 1996

Dugal, J. (1996b), 'Human Being and Human Doing', in *Proceedings of the 1996 Creativity in Education Conference*, The Open University (available from Anna Craft, The Open University School of Education, Walton Hall, Milton Keynes, MK7 6AA

Dyer, G.C. (1995), 'Developing a Family Declaration of Interdependence: A Methodology for Systems Design within a Small Social Unit, *Systems Research*, Vol. 12, 3

Galton, M., Simon, B. (1980a), *Progress and Performance in the Primary Classroom*, London: Routledge & Kegan Paul

Galton, M., Simon, B., Croll, P. (1980b), *Inside the Primary Classroom*, London: Routledge & Kegan Paul

Galton, M. and Williamson, J. (1992), *Group work in the primary school*, London: Routledge

Horiuchi, Y. (1994), 'Social Systems Navigation: A Multi-Layer Ideal System. In Brady, B. and Peeno, L. (eds) (1996), *New Systems Thinking and Action for the 21st Century*, Louisville, International Society for the Systems Sciences

Kimberley, C. (1996), 'Making the Impossible Possible', in *Proceedings of the 1996 Creativity in Education Conference,* The Open University (available from Anna Craft, The Open University School of Education, Walton Hall, Milton Keynes, MK7 6AA

Webb, R. (1993), *Eating the Elephant Bit by Bit: The National Curriculum at Key Stage 1 and 2*: Final report of research commissioned by the Association of Teachers and Lecturers (ATL), London: ATL Publishers

White, M. (1991) *The Benefits of Circle Time,* a 28 page booklet available for £ 4.50 from Murray White, 5 Ferry Path Road, Cambridge, CB4 1HB

White, M. (1992), *Self-Esteem, its meaning and value in schools: a step by step guide to conducting circle time in the classroom, packs A and B,* Dustable: Folens

White, M. (1994a), *Raising Self-Esteem: 50 activities,* Dunstable: Folens

White, M. (1994b), *Picture This: Guided Imagery for Circle Times,* Dunstable: Folens

White, M. (ed) (1995), *Self-Esteem Solutions,* Dunstable: Folens

White, M. (1996), 'Circle Time - What it is, how it works and why children love it', in *Proceedings of the 1996 Creativity in Education Conference,* The Open University (available from Anna Craft, The Open University School of Education, Walton Hall, Milton Keynes, MK7 6AA

Wragg, E. C. and Brown, G. (1993), *Explaining,* London: Routledge

Wragg, E. C. and Dunne, R. (1994), *Effective Teaching,* London: Routledge

Chapter 9

Challenges to Vision and Creativity

Anna Craft and Jana Dugal

In parts of this chapter, we draw on the Creativity in Education Programme which began in 1995, a part of which is a postgraduate course on Creativity in Education taught by The Institute for Creativity and accredited by The Open University.

We look at some of the structures and beliefs which can challenge vision in education. We look first at blocks to individual creativity for teachers and learners, and then look at some wider systems issues which can challenge creativity.

Finally we look at some strategies for giving voice to your own vision. Dotted throughout the chapter are practical processes for use by individuals or groups.

'I'm stuck'

How often do you hear this, either from yourself or from the children? Feeling stuck, or blocked, is very common in creative activity. Also very common is the feeling that it has 'been done to us', and, as a consequence, it can be sorted out for us.

We begin in this chapter from the perspective that many of our blocks are actually self-imposed, and that we ourselves hold the key to discovering how far the blocks are internal, external, real or imagined. Some of us allow ourselves to believe that external forces will never allow us to to exercise creativity. But is this really so?

Cast your eye over this list of suggested activities.

- listen to one or more of Beethoven's late string quartets (No's 13, 14 15 and 16)

- read poetry which has been written in the last ten years

- spend some time out of doors in reflection

- read a specified article on promoting reflection in learning

- write an algebraic formula (which may represent a real-life scenario)

- write down a dream you have had

- read an article by Fryer and Collings (1991) on teachers' views of creativity

- use whatever means are appropriate to you, find your way to a new place

- think of a way to introduce yourself to someone you do not know

Which leapt out at you as appealing? Which as boring? Which as impossible? What feelings were evoked in you as you read the list? Which activity, if any, would you choose to do?

The list was developed for the course on Creativity in Education mentioned at the start of the chapter. It is designed to help individuals to explore internal inhibitors to their creativity, and to explore some of the domains in which they are happiest being creative.

Challenges to creativity from within oneself: internal inhibitors

Learned habits can inhibit us. What we value may be what we do not need. Shallcross (1981) lists the following internal inhibitors:

* assumed expectations of other people,
* failure to be aware of all available information,
* lack of effort or laziness,
* assumed or self-imposed boundaries or limitations,
* mind sets,

* mind sets,
* rigidity or inflexibility...
* fear of failure or of taking risks,
* fear of ridicule,
* reliance on authority or following patterns of behaviour set by others,
* routine,
* comfort,
* familiarity,
* a need for things to be orderly all the time,
* superstition and acceptance of fate, heredity or one's station in life.'

Source: Shallcross, 1981, p 65-66

Shallcross's list includes overlapping and repeating items, and of course is not exhaustive. We would add to it,

* lack of practice in making choices,
* workaholism and other addictions,
* fear of change,
* a wish to control,
* fear of not being good enough,
* inexperience in acknowledging existing achievements,
* lack of awareness of how others perceive one's actions,
* cynicism, or practised refusal/inflexibility.

Where do learned habits come from?

Becoming more aware of some of the things which hold you back from vision and creativity is one one step towards 'getting unstuck'. Later in this chapter we suggest some practical strategies for freeing up your own creativity (see 'Process and Choice').

Internal inhibitors are not the only ones we face, particularly when contemplating system-level change. Global, trans-national and national society provides the context for our creative impulses, and it is a complex and contradictory one, which we now turn to.

Challenges to creativity from society

Questions and suppression

Creativity involves asking questions. Consequently, we can expect creativity to be consciously suppressed in certain contexts - and historically it has been, as philosopher Kieran Egan (1992) has charted. His analysis of the marginalisation of imagination and creativity demonstrates ways in which imagination and creativity have since the time of the ancient Greeks, represented a 'rebellion against divine order' (1992: 13). Thus, he argues, the notion 'in the imagination' has attracted disapproval and has been considered to be a mimicking of divine capability. Although the Romantic imagination reversed some of the negativity associated with imagination and creativity through the development of the Romantic Arts, nevertheless the centrality of imagination and creativity in all domains of knowledge and for all people, has only toward the end of the 20th century, become critical to everyday lives.

The end of the 20th Century: creativity as essential to every day lives

Individual and corporate creativity/imagination have now become a topic of study by cognitive psychologists, philosophers, educationalists, and management experts alike (Stern, 1992). As argued in this book, the end of the twentieth century is witnessing a massive shift in attitude to and importance of, creativity and imagination in everyday lives and domains of knowledge. We need transformation, at both personal and system level.

The fragmentary nature of our postmodern existence means that in many ways the mores and shared traditions are mixed and confused. Multiple possibilities exist for us in adopting, for example, spiritual, social, economic and technological identities and actions. In many arenas we have no models to follow and are having to work out what the possibilities are as we go along.

The family is an example. 40% of children now live in families where one parent has found a new partnership. That is nearly half of all children, who now belong to, or have experience of, more than one family!

The spiritual arena provides another example. Although there has been a collapse of participation from the established churches and religions represented in Britain over the last twenty years, there has at the same time been a massive rise in seekers of their own brand of spirituality.

We have found continual references to spiritual awakening in the Creativity in Education Programme (Craft and Lyons, 1996). This is not in the form of participation in established churches but is rather in the nature of spiritual enquiry. Other sources suggest that the quest for spiritual existence and expression is an important part of daily existence for many people, as Virginia F Harris (1996) has highlighted. The immense variety in self help and learning resource books also provide evidence of the quest for spiritual and personal meaning.

Such seeking has been called, by Michael Ignatieff (presenter of the 1997 Radio 4 series entitled '20/20; a View of the Century'), 'pick'n'mix' spirituality, drawing often on major world religions including Buddhism, as well as tribal belief systems such as those of the North American Indians. There is far less adherence to certainty within spiritual life, and a far greater tendency for individuals, particularly the young, to seek their own path, laying it down as they walk it.

Alongside this huge shift to choosing one's own way, is of course a return to forms of religious fundamentalism within some communities, even though these are numerically in the minority. We discuss some other examples of contradictions in our society, later on in this chapter.

Paradoxically, whilst the certitude of the organisation of established religions collapses, certainty in the path of seeking, rises. It seems to us that creativity and spiritual enquiry are often in the same arena and come from the same foundation, or source. In other words, both are forms of 'seeking'. Individual development seems us to be attempting to develop another forum for spiritual purpose, which is not (although does not necessarily exclude) the established world religions.

Creativity, enabling the individual to walk with personal reflection and accountability, can do much, in our view, to change the cynicism that bites the heel of the new millenium - and it opens the way to vision.

'Listening' to your own reactions Close your eyes and take a few deep breaths. Listen to and notice your own reactions to what you have read in this chapter so far. If it helps you to notice your thoughts by writing them down, do so.

Your reaction to the 'listening' exercise above provides you with information. Your reaction may, at present, be one of excitement. Of inspiration. Or, you may have found yourself having a reaction of frustration. Even of boredom, or of cynicism. Whatever you are experiencing gives you information about your beliefs about choices available to you.

Choice and belief

For now we want to look at choice, and access to it. There is, of course, differentiation of access to some choices, and you may believe that the richest and most powerful members of society have much more choice, than the poorest and least powerful. Some of these issues are geographically and chance-specific. For example, having choice over one's future economic role in society may be much less applicable to a thirteen year old boy living in Hackney than it is to a boy of the same age living in Hampstead. And you may believe that a woman of thirty with no children who lives in a two-income family is much more likely to have access to communications, learning, the market and entertainment through information technology, than a woman of the same age living alone with three small children and no earned income of her own.

What we are suggesting is that perceptions of these differences in access to creativity may in turn be embedded in the beliefs and potential barriers thrown up by the social, economic, gender, geographic and ethnic context of each individual.

What follow are two processes for bringing possibility thinking to bear on the choices which inspire your outlook and therefore your general activity. These processes can be worked through individually and in groupwork.

A means for unwrapping cynicism: the essential you

This is a very simple process to illuminate the qualities of your nature that best work for you and that can therefore inspire your work environment. We use the word 'essential' to draw on both

* features and dimensions of you that you value highly
* what you feel to be your 'essence' - ie the nature of you.

Ask yourself the following questions, designed to help you to disover both the qualities which are essential to you and also elements of your own essence. When answering them, hold in mind your work environment.

* What is essential to you?
* What is essential ABOUT you?
* How can you express these qualities?
* Who are you essential to? and with?
* Where are you essential?

If you are working in a group, if you can, see what others perceive in you.

Right and wrong: how you perceive your relationships

This second process is designed to support you in exploring your current perceptions of important relationships in your life, and how you perceive 'right' and 'wrong' within them.

It is designed to encourage possibility thinking and to enable you to discern new means of creating relationships. For example, if in your perception of your own history, Mum was often right and you often felt wrong, how much of that old habit do you replay in your current relationships?

By filling in the framework provided in Table 1, you may discover a range of roles you are playing. This may enable you to look at new possibilities available to you for transcending old habits. The filled-in example which follows is based on a response in the Creativity in Education programme, to demonstrate how you might use it.

Both of the processes above were designed to help you explore how you perceive choices in your own life. For in our view, creativity and vision come from a place of belief in one's potential to make choices.

A society of contradictions

We live in a society of contradictions: on the one hand choice, possibility, change and growth are seen as necessary and overtly encouraged. Our existence revolves around what Smart (1993) has called 'relational values' rather than absolute ones, partly because of the continual state of flux in which society exists.

On the other hand, there is an increase in uniformity at the level of the market, as Ritzer (1993) has identified, in what he has called 'McDonaldization', in other words, the domination of homogenous produces, work routines and technologies such as one finds in the McDonald's chain of hamburger stores. With this increase in uniformity, comes a set of rigidly adhered to organisational values and rules - indeed there is even a McDonald's University, which teaches employees the values and beliefs of the chain.

It has been argued (Craft, 1995) that there is some parallel beween the values-uniformity implied within the McDonald's set up and chains like it, and the discernable political attempt to control and hold still within education. The modes of doing so include the centralized school curriculum and arrangements for assessing learning of it, and an increased emphasis on managerialism, which is well documented (Avis et al, 1996).

If we look at creativity in education then, we see a need on the one hand for teachers to become

Table 1: Perceptions of relationships

NAME (people in your life)	WHO IS RIGHT AND WHO IS WRONG?	WHAT I DO TO MAINTAIN IT?	CHOICE NOW AVAILABLE TO ME

NAME	WHO IS RIGHT AND WHO IS WRONG?	WHAT I DO TO MAINTAIN IT?	CHOICE NOW AVAILABLE TO ME
Dad	He's right, I'm wrong	I behave as the underdog	Forgive or confront him
Mum	I'm right, she's wrong	I behave in a powerful manner, I am intellectual, I am supportive and make it 'OK' for her by pleasing her.	Talk to her
Rob (my brother)	Sometimes I am right and he is wrong, sometimes he is right and I am wrong	I compete with him	Withdraw
Men	They are right, I am wrong	I choose relationships with arrogant men, whom I find attractive for some reason!	Pray!!

increasingly experts in fostering creativity, and on the other an attempt to crush all artistry from the profession and to reduce teaching to a technicist activity.

Other society level challenges to creativity and vision include the role and mode of communications - the mass media. Philip Gammage (1996) has spoken of the tendency of the mass media to 'gobbetize' information - it could also be argued that the media is capable of misinformation, purely by dint of what is left out, and the simplistic ways in which complex issues are presented.

Two recent examples of this include the recent live TV debate on the future of the monarchy, in which the speakers for and against scarcely got the opportunity to lay out their cases before a lively studio debate began in which heated opinions were given the same weight as carefully constructed arguments, questions to trigger voting were biased, and the voting procedures themselves open to question. Another example concerns a recent trip which Anna made to New York, just before Christmas 1996. She was struck at the paucity of news on the television - and the inclusion of news items such as the shortage of 'Tickle me Elmo' cuddly toys in the stores right across the USA. This was lead story on several news programmes, alongside the hostages being held in the Japanese embassy in Peru. The question raised for her was, 'Why was this sales story considered to be news at all?'

Respond to the Tickle Me Elmo story

How do you respond to Anna's question, 'Why was this sales story considered to be news at all?' Jot down your thoughts, giving yourself no more than five minutes to do so.

Now look at your responses. What values underpin your views? Again, give yourself no more than five minutes to jot down your ideas.

If you are working with others, share your reactions as a group.

In thinking about what values underpin your reactions, you may find it helpful to read these initial reactions

which came from some of the educators involved in the Creativity in Education Project:

News has to support sales in the United States, unlike here

News items like that are specially designed to draw in child viewers - it is a commercial gimmick.

Maybe there was no other big news story that day.

It's good entertainment.

Sales in America means success.

All children have the right to have stories which affect them represented in adult news programmes.

Christmas is about sales.

TV must tell domestic news stories.

Within these responses are a variety of value positions including cynical, 'naive', descriptive, positive/ appreciative, and a concern for children's rights for representation. The educators who generated this list had a heated debate about which perspective most closely represented the programme makers' intentions. The point of this exercise is to highlight the different, and contradictory, lenses through which individuals interpret the same representation of the world through the mass media.

The 'Tickle Me Elmo' story also highlights another contradiction. Television is an immensely creative form of mass media, in both its presentation and the effect which it has on viewers. However it has the potential to simplify and mis-represent. Although it is a medium capable of stimulating creative, thoughtful responses, it has the potential to close down debate entirely. The same phenomenon can be observed in the film industry, in glossy magazines, in tabloid (and to a lesser extent, broadsheet) newspapers, and in the booming CD-Rom market place. However, the fact that parts of the the media may portray the 'market as God' does not have to lead us into acceptance of this proposition - witness the different reactions to the

'Tickle Me Elmo' exercise.

The deification of the market is another of the contradictions which we live with. Innovation is critical to increased competitiveness in business. The challenge is to invent, re-package or re-conceptualise ideas and products just as the previous one peaks, with the result that we are sucked into a continuous cycle of invention and sale. Thus living in a market economy where goods are bought and sold on the basis of want rather than need, with market values determined by factors such as scarcity and abundance, drives us in to a need for creative activity. Peter Skinner (1996) has called the constant need for innovation in the workplace as 'mentafacture' - production by brain, and stylofacture - the production of lifestyle possibilities. Innovation in this context can be seen as the successful exploitation of new ideas.

And yet, as the marketplace drives this creative activity it can also dull our capability to see beyond the framework of values in which we are innovating. It makes it more difficult for us to see the impact of our innovations on the globe, its peoples, creatures, seascapes, landscapes and vegetation.

So, the values of our society can be seen as providing both inducements and barriers to creating, and more importantly, to the ways in which we perceive our creations.

Facts and beliefs: live challenges

This process is about separating out your beliefs from the reality of your life. Belief is a perspective on truth.

First, note down three facts about your professional life.

Then, note down the beliefs which surround each of these facts.

You may find it helpful to look at this example drawn from the Creativity in Education Project.

Fact: *Mr Young is my boss.*
Belief: *He doesn't support me.*

Fact: *I teach a group of twenty-five Y5 children.*
Belief: *As a group they are quite easy to work with.*
Fact: *I stay behind often to change wall displays at school.*
Belief: *The wall displays are a motivating part of the learning environment for the children.*

The process is one which can be used to help you explore what beliefs of your own might surround some of the live issues in your professional life. Having identified your beliefs you can ask yourself what values underpin them. It is these which either induce or block your creativity.

Summing up so far:

In the first part of this chapter we have suggested that our underpinning beliefs about our personal lives and the society which surrounds us, may foster or block our own creativity. We have named a number of possible internal inhibitors proposed by Shallcross, which cover, broadly, our attitudes to:

* risk;
* role in relation to others;
* information;
* flexibility;
* change;
* will and determinism.

To Shallcross's internal inhibitors, we added a number of our own, which covered, broadly:
  * experience in exercising will;
  * addictive traits;
  * fear (of change, of not being good enough, of not being in control);
  * insensitivity in relationship with others, and
  * cynicism.

We explored some societal sources of learned habits which suppress creativity, including some of the contradictions of post-modern living. In particular we examined the fragmentation and multiple possibilities in our lives, played out in many arenas: the spiritual, social, economic, technological. This co-exists with the contrasting consolidation of fundamentalism and uniformity in each of these arenas.

Summary (continued):

We looked at choice and belief, suggesting that our perceptions of the choices available to us are based on beliefs. Whilst we may not be able to alter some of the given inequalities in access to choice in society, we can however explore other belief positions. We offered a number of examples and practical exercises to support this process in the context of societal contradictions.

In the next part of the chapter we look at some of the practical challenges involved in transforming education through vision.

The challenge of transforming education through vision

Education greatly needs vision. As Michael Barber puts it eloquently in his recent book (1996), we are faced with global challenge, as well as moral collapse and confusion. In addition, we are faced with poor comparison with our competitor countries such as France, Germany and Japan, in terms of how well educated our young people are (outside the top 20%) when they leave school. There are increasing anxieties about the basic skills attainment of young people. Aside from concerns voiced by OFSTED (1996) and other bodies such as the Secondary Heads Association (1996), the Basic Skills Agency reported recently that among adults aged twenty one, 15% have problems with literacy, and 20% with numeracy.

These problems form part of yet another set of contradictions; they lie alongside 'successes', which include much higher achievement in GCSEs, A levels and GNVQs, the increasing trend of girls out-performing boys at all levels, as well as higher staying-on rates (though these are balanced against changes in the economy which mean jobs are scarce and incentives to leave full time education are therefore fewer than they were).

A further contradiction is that alongside the increased staying-on rates, more and more children, particularly boys in their early teens onward, are truanting from school, or being excluded. Indeed as Tim Brighouse,

Chief Education Officer of Birmingham, pointed out at the 1994 Council of Local Authorities Conference, 'the pattern of exclusion, having been almost exclusively confined to Year 11 (age sixteen) youngsters ten years ago, has shifted first to Year 11 and Year 10, then to Year 11, Year 10 and Year 9, and finally until now there is a strong representation of years 11, 10, 9 and 8 among those permanently excluded from the school in which they were orignally enrolled in Year 7. Moreover, the overall numbers have escalated through that 10-year period.'

As Michael Barber (1996) points out, alongside the truanting, or the 'disappeared' are the disaffected. Quoting from the Keele University surveys of 30,000 children in secondary schools, he claims that pupil disruption, bullying and noise affect a third of respondents. He suggests 'it is necessary to reach the depressing conclusion that a minority, perhaps 10 - 15 per cent nationally, but much more numerous in some particular schools, are disrupting education for the majority of pupils and impairing the quality of teacher-pupil relationships throughout many schools.' (ibid, p78-79). He also points out that boredom and lack of motivation affect huge numbers of children.

Although the Keele data is from secondary education, we quote it here to emphasise that we need a form of educating which enables all children to exercise imagination and creativity through engaged learning throughout their schooling and in a way which has relevance to their lives, now and in the future. Can you with all certainty say that all of the children with whom you have contact, feel motivated and that school is relevant for them? We have a need to jump beyond the cultural revolution which was imposed on schools in the late 1980s, and beyond the institutional constraints formed by the type of mass-schooling system which we operate as part of now, to something which is more likely to equip learners for the uncertainties and skill demands in life.

Doing it differently, not doing it more

We need to step outside of the contradictions, to go beyond 'improvement' or 'effectiveness'. In terms of creativity, we need to look beyond fostering creative approaches for the same ends, to how we could do it differently, at whatever level we are working.

There are plenty of suggestions already around - for example, Barber and Brighouse's proposals for long-term associateships from the local community, in order to help keep teachers up to date with change in knowledge and its application, and the need to provide more teaching assistants at the level of 'para-professionals', the possibility of learning accounts for teachers and much more flexible times and places of work for teachers and pupils (Barber and Brighouse, 1992).

Barber (1996) has proposed the 'Individual Learning Promise' which should be a commitment to learning agreed through a partnership of the pupil, the school and the pupil's parents, where the individual's progress is planned, implemented and reviewed. Small independent centres such as the New Learning Centre in North London are already working on these lines, alongside schools.

John Adcock (1994) too has suggested a model of teaching and learning based on the personal tutor supported by media resource centres, and personal choice on the part of children. Roland Meighan (1997) has suggested home learning is a powerful precursor to the next learning system.

And thousands of parents are now educating their children at home, supported in the UK by organisations such as Education Otherwise. Education at home is increasingly common in Europe, North America and also in Australasia, and this is well documented (Thomas, 1994b, Meighan, 1995). Not only this, but there is increasing evidence that early intellectual development happens through everyday conversations (Tizard and Hughes, 1984, Rogoff, 1990). According to research undertaken by Alan Thomas (1992, 1994a), formalised teaching sessions for children educated in the home seem to have little difference in effectiveness from the 'natural apprenticeship' model which tends to be used in infancy. The suggestion from Thomas's work is that to be effective, learning may not need to take place in the 'classroom'. And as Meighan (1995) documents, the intellectual achievement and social skills of home educated children are repeatedly demonstrated to be excellent.

Home schoolers are not necessarily isolated, according to Marchant (1993) who investigated the way in which 185 families from 37 states in the USA were regularly exchanging information and ideas on a regular basis via their home computers - without ever having met one another face to face. In this respect computers have a huge amount to offer to visions of education, although problems of privilege, wealth, the educational status of parents and social class all combine to mean that home education is probably never going to be an option for the majority of parents and children.

The authors of this chapter have a vision of a system of education which would co-exist with free day care from 8am until 7pm, in which children would have both an entitlement to learn (and the resource to support it; a notion also proposed by the National Commission on Education - 1995), and also far more choice about what, how and when they undertook it, and thus they would enter in to learning contracts of finite length. Consequently the job of being a teacher would involve much greater flexibility, and probably smaller numbers of pupils.

A similar model is proposed by Barber (1996) who suggests 'Policy makers will need to begin to think of education as having three strands:
 * *learning at school;*
 * *learning in organised out-of-school locations; and*
 * *learning at home.'*
(Barber, 1996, p 259)

The point is, we need to do it differently.

And at the heart of the need to do it differently rather than doing it more, is the idea summed up in this old Hebrew proverb:

Do not confine your children to your own learning for they were born in another time.

Source: Meighan, R. (1994), *The Freethinkers' Guide to the Educational Universe*

We a need new paradigm for creating vision in education, which allows us to step outside of the contradictions, to a space which enables us to create with vision, from compassion. It means applying our creativity to create new frameworks. It means drawing on our creative impulses from a different level. In the next section we draw on the notion of trusting what is 'implicate', a term coined by scientists Bohm and Peat (1989).

Trusting what is implicate

For each aspect of our lives we have everyday, 'working' theories and explanations. So, you may have a theories about who has authority in your school, or what it is possible to achieve in fostering children's creativity. These theories are born, largely, of experience: our own and what we have learned about from others. What we take to be the reality of our lives, including the limits to change, is sometimes called 'the explicate world'. And it is supported by our working theories of action.

But underneath our explicate world, is what Bohm and Peat call an 'implicate world' (1989). Our implicate understandings are often far more complex than our explicate ones, and they can be difficult to articulate. We have all experienced moments when we are frustrated by being unable to fully explain a complicated idea. What is really important about implicate ideas is that they have generative potential. In other words, the flash of understanding which is so hard to explain, holds within it many possible unfoldments.

If you visualise how you would like to see transformation occur within the education system, you may find yourself getting stuck. One reason for this may be that the explicate order, the here-and-now, supported by your theories of why it is as it is, has a powerful hold. The here-and-now provides resistance to generative, new possibilities. You may find yourself saying "Well, I think children should not have to attend school if they don't want to", but then you may find yourself saying "but who would look after them and how would they learn anything?" Our experience of what we already know, provides all kinds of reasons

to resist change - and the more complex our experience, the greater our resistance.

Bohm and Peat argue that we need more access to the implicate orders which underly our explicate ones, because they are the source of generative ideas, in other words, of our creativity. They argue that we need a new kind of 'creative surge' at the end of the 20th century, which will enable us to find ways of breaking out of rigidity. We would argue, with Bohm and Peat, that we now need to foster an order of creativity which extends into social organisation, science, culture and consciousness. What this means is allowing our implicate and generative selves to have a voice, because that is where our creative intelligence lies.

The complexity of the problems which surround society of which our education system forms a part (we would argue the heart) does challenge our creative intelligence greatly. A growing inequitable distribution of wealth within prosperous society, environmental destruction, revolutions in technology, spirituality, management and communications, all bring huge creative possibilities and huge uncertainty regarding the nature of existence, work and human action in the world.

As teachers we have a critical role in shaping a vision for educating which responds with compassion to the uncertainty and instability which grows around us.

A connectivist approach

Although we acknowledge the societal barriers and challenges to creativity in education, and Barber's suggestion that we require 'visionary and assertive leadership' (Barber, 1996 p291), we also believe that the action of individuals makes a difference. And, that as individuals develop so do the institutions of which they are part. But only if we each take our development and our vision in to our workplaces.

Vision at work

What follows are two processes to encourage creative solutions at work.

Choosing your status

Actors, when learning a new role, often play a status game where each player performs his character in high or low status.

This process, drawn from the acting exercise, is similar to the one about relationships, earlier in the chapter.

Divide a piece of paper in to columns, and along the top of the paper, the people you currently work with. In the second row, identify your perception of their status to you. In the third, identify your perception of your status in relation to them. In the fourth, consider what possibilities there are for change, and respond to the question: 'what is now possible?'

By discerning how you act to maintain an unequal balance new possibilities can open up for change in the relationship. Choose.

For example, table 2 shows one filled in by an educator who trialled the process.

Fill in your sheet with your own choices. When appropriate get support for your actions. Remember, the solution won't be aggressive!

Cynicism and its effect on your life

Cynicism is perhaps the most negating of human activities. Its origin lies deep within our own personal disappointments and needs immediate addressing. Cynicism acts as a punishment on all new ideas, and although ironic and sometimes witty, it can dismantle all sorts of opportunities for transformation.

Here are some questions. Devised by Jana, they are designed to stimulate an enquiry into the nature of cynicism. By recognising the effect of cynicism on your professional life, what possible choices now exist for transormation?

How do I use my cynicism at work?

What language do I use to maintain it?

What is possible when I stop being cynical?

Whose fault is it?

Table 2, Choosing your status		
NAME	**DAVE**	**PETE**
THEIR STATUS TO ME	Dominant	Low
MY STATUS TO THEM	Demeaned	High
WHAT DO I DO?	I am a pleaser and a maker of tea	I shine
WHAT DO I DO? CHOICE NOW AVAILABLE TO ME	By recognising Dave's own security I can redevelop the relationship	Keep shining, find abundant ways to nourish him

Cynicism process, continued

What choices are available to me?

How can I create relationship without blame?

Who do I blame? Avoid? Please? in order to get my own way?
What, and who, needs forgiving?

What is compassion? How can my compassion speak for me?
What conversation is possible with compassion?

Jana writes: *'I have found these questions immensely helpful when working in schools where a number of problems had led to immense self-defeat. In one school the Head was isolated and tyrannical, in one the choices for teachers seemed slim and under resourced. Each school had evidence of deep cynical response as a survival mechanism. Staff and schools alike, maintained a policy of mutual hostility. When we recognise we are each accountable for this happening, then we can choose to maintain it, or change. The minute we choose a change, all things are possible.*

Transformation, through vision, outlines the way out of negativity, often stating that the negative belief is just that - a belief. Recognising this, and acting from a new place of assurance and conviction, leads to transformation'

Practising

Picture Rachel's challenge:

Having trained to teach infants, Rachel taught the Reception class in an inner London school for two years. When a colleague retired, she had the opportunity to teach children aged 9 and 10. She took up the challenge feeling nervous and ill-equipped. The advice her head teacher gave her was, 'Act the part and the rest will follow'. This made little sense to Rachel but she invented a persona and tried it out for the first few weeks. She was a great success with the children who found her blend of high expectations, discipline and warmth both

encouraging and stimulating. Years later, when she eventually moved on from that school, children and parents petitioned her to stay.

This may be a familiar story to you. Practising 'in role' is one way of overcoming fear, blocks and barriers. Having a go is essential to taking creative action. Whatever the outcomes of your own actions to transform children's learning, at whatever level, what will keep you going is the engine phrase, 'what if?'

Now picture Steve, an LEA adviser and OFSTED Inspector for geography.

Steve has responsibility for inspecting families who educate at home. A growing number of parents in his LEA are taking this decision. He is concerned at the exhaustion among many teachers whom he meets, and their lack of creative energy. He finds himself constantly under pressure to 'perform' in his job, as almost all of the services which he provides to schools are now 'bought back' by them. Thus his continued employment depends on how the teachers and schools perceive his worth. As an OFSTED Inspector in schools in his own and other LEAs, he feels concerned at the pressures the experience creates for whole school communities and wonders whether it is appropriate to do this. He feels his heartfelt concerns, to support and inspire teachers and children, are under great pressure. His instinctual reaction is to gradually begin to stand outside the mainstream frame. Step by step, he has begun to introduce in-service courses which address more personal issues for teachers of geography, and he has started to involve himself in a number of national initiatives focusing on vision and creativity in education. Although he still feels these are early days, he is discovering other staff from within his LEA who are involved in these wider initiatives, and who want to create a different vision for their school, their area of responsibility in the LEA, or their own working life. In short, he is practising. He's starting to say 'what if?' for more and more of his time.

Re-engineering

Steve's story tells the tale of what Hammer and Champy (1993) call 're-engineering'. Describing the business revolution, they define re-engineering a company as 'tossing aside old systems and starting over. It involves going back to the beginning and inventing a better way of doing work'....

> What does your own story of re-engineering education look like? Who is it focused on? What are you prepared and able to toss aside at present? You might like to take a few minutes to write it down, to date.

A part of the whole

We have been talking about re-engineering our conceptions of education in order to foster greater creativity. As we re-engineer our ideas in one part of our lives, other aspects are affected.

Our lives are made up of many arenas. When we experience success or defeat in one part of our life, it can influence other parts of our lives. What we need to do in overcoming blocks to our creativity is to both analyse the block and synthesise our experience of it with the other segments of our life.

Shallcross (1981) describes a technique for doing this, which goes like this:

Divide up a sheet of paper in to six columns, as follows:

Role

Major Goal

Major Obstacle

Usual Result

Desired Result

Alternative Behaviou

In the first column, write down all of the roles which you are aware of taking on in your life. Include both the obvious and the not-so-obvious. As you complete the second column, match the goals with each role which you have listed, along ... then complete the other columns except for the last one, by working down or along, whichever seems easier to you.

Table 3 shows one completed by an educator involved in the Creativity in Education Project.

Consider what information the chart reveals to you. You will probably find that in most roles your major goal has obstacles which are easily overcome. However for those where the obstacles are problems,

Table 3 chapter 9

Role	Major Goal	Major Obstacle	Usual Result	Desired Result	Alternative Behaviour
Teacher	To inspire	Exhaustion (mine)	Resentment (in me)	Energy (in me)	Do less, rest more
Parent	To care	Conflicting demands (work and home)	Running round in circles	Time to parent	Explore options for jobshare (financial/prac)
Rescuer	To solve problems of 'victims'	Victim resistance!	Frustration (in me)	To feel valued	Find value elsewhere?

you need to do some thinking. Shallcross suggests that for these you apply the following questions - and then if possible, talk your answers through with someone who knows you well:

Is the goal one I have a real investment in?

Is the obstacle real?

Is the obstacle to do with my attitudes?

Is the obstacle external to me?

Is the obstacle internal to me?

Does the same obstacle appear more than once on my chart?

What you may find is that an obstacle is non-existent. Or, that another, once noticed, is not difficult to overcome. Go on then to the final column, to think of possible ways of changing your own behaviour so that you get your desired result. Then - try one of them out.

What you may find is that trying out a behaviour in one aspect of your life brings a change in other aspects. It is important to remember too, that nothing succeeds in giving confidence to behave differently more than actually practising it.

Finally....

We hope you enjoy the enquiry and continue to use 'creative process' as a resource in your transformational work.

Summing up on developing vision in education

In exploring the challenges involved in transforming education through vision, we have suggested that what we need is to do it differently rather than doing it more; to go beyond 'improvement' to looking at how we might educate in a different way or ways. We mentioned some which have already been proposed:

* Barber's 'Individual Learning Promise';
* Adcock's personal tutorial method;
* home learning (which many thousands are now exploring) and which Meighan suggests is the precursor to the next learning system, and
* our own model of communitiy learning centres combining care and education (also proposed by the National Commission on Education and similar to Barber's model of three-strand learning: at school, out-of-school and at home).

In creating new frameworks for learning and teaching with children aged 3 - 13, we have suggested we need to draw on our creative impulses from a different level. Drawing on Bohm and Peat, Hammer and Champy, workshop processes undertaken with educators and teachers' classroom practice, we have proposed:

* trusting the implicate; giving greater credence to intuitive understandings and ideas which we suggest offer generativepotential even if we find them hard to articulate.

* a connectivist approach, which means bringing our vision to work, being prepared to move through cynicism to compassion, and to 'have a go'.

In doing so we have suggested that vision in education can be seen as 're-engineering' rather than as 'reform' and that one's own vision for education is locked in to other arenas in one's life, which may throw up blocks to our creativity. We have proposed a process for examining these.

References

Adcock, J. (1994), In Place of Schools: A Novel Plan for the 21st Century, London: New Education Press Ltd

Avis, J., Bloomer, M., Esland, G.M.., Gleeson, D. and Hodkinson, P. (1996) *Knowledge and Nationhood: education, politics and work* London, Cassell

Barber, M. (1996), *The Learning Game: Arguments for an Education Revolution*, London: Cassell

Barber, M., Brighouse, T. (1992), *Partners in Change: Enhancing the Teaching Profession*, London: IPPR

Bohm, D. and Peat, P.D. (1989), *Science, Order and Creativity*, London: Routledge

Craft, A. (1995), 'Cross-curricular Integration and the Construction of Self', in Ahier, J. and Ross, A. (eds) (1995), *The Social Subjects Within the Curriculum: Children's Social Learning in the National Curriculum*, London: Falmer

Craft, A., Lyons, T. (1997), *Creativity in Education Seminar Network Occasional Paper 1: Nourishing the Educator*, Milton Keynes: The Open University (available from Anna Craft or Hazel Sampson on 01908 652652)

Egan, K. (1992), *Imagination in Teaching and Learning*, Routledge, London

Fryer, M., Collings, J.A. (1991), 'Teachers' views about creativity', *British Journal of Educational Psychology*, 61, pp207-219

Gammage, P. (1996), 'Barriers to Creativity', *Keynote Lecture at Conference on Creativity in Education, June 1996*, The Open University, London

Hammer, M., Champy, J. (1993), *Re-engineering the Corporation: Manifesto for a Business Revolution*, London: Brearley Publishing

Harris, Virginia F. (1996), Speech at *Conference on Spirituality and Healing in Medicine (2)*, Harvard Medical School and the Mind Body Medical Institute, Deaconness Hospital Boston, December 1996.

Meighan, R. (1994), *The Freethinkers' Guide to the Educational Universe*, Nottingham: Educational Heretics Press

Meighan, R. (1995), 'Home-Based Education Effectiveness Research and Some of its Implications, *Educational Review*, Vol. 47, No. 3

Meighan, R. (1997), *The Next Learning System*, Nottingham: Educational Heretics Press

National Commission on Education (1995) *Learning to Succeed: A Radical Look at Education Today and a Strategy for the Future - a follow-up report*, London: NCE

OFSTED, *The Teaching of Reading in 45 Inner London Primary Schools*, Ref: HMR/27/96/DS, London: OFSTED

Ritzer, G. (1993), *The McDonaldization of Society: An Investigation Into the Changing Character of Contemporary Social Life*, Newbury Park, CA: Pine Forge Press

Rogoff, B. (1990), *Apprenticeship in Thinking: Cognitive Development in Social Context*, New York: Oxford University Press

Secondary Heads' Association (1996), *SHA Survey of Intake Tests in Secondary Schools*, Leicester: SHA

Shallcross, D.J. (1981), *Teaching Creative Behaviour: How to Teach Creativity to Children of All Ages*, Englewood Cliffs, New Jersey: Prentice-Hall

Skinner, P. (1996), 'Innovation and Creativity: education and the future of work', *Keynote Lecture at Conference on Creativity in Education, June 1996*, The Open University, London

Smart, B. (1993), *Postmodernity*, London: Routledge

Stern, S. (1992), 'The Relationship between Human Resource Development, Development and Corporate Creativity in Japan', *Human Resource Development Quarterly*, Vol. 3, No 3, Fall 1992, Jossey-Bass Publishers

Thomas, A. (1992), Individualised Teaching, *Oxford Review of Education*, Vol. 18, No. 1, 1992

Thomas, A. (1994a), Conversational Learning, *Oxford Review of Education*, Vol. 20, No. 1, 1994

Thomas, A. (1994b), 'The Quality of Learning Experienced by Children who are Educated at Home', presentation given at *British Psychological Society Annual Conference*, Brighton, 1994

Tizard, B., Hughes, M. (1984), *Children Learning at Home and in School*, London: Fontana

POSTSCRIPT

Humane Creativity in the Classroom

Time is short and the task is urgent. Auschwitz is the prime example of what happens when technology is harnessed to evil. Evil is real. So is good. There is a choice and we are not so much chosen as choosers. Life is holy. All life, mine and yours and that of those who came before us and the life of those after us.
Hugo Gryn (1930-1996)

These words, spoken by Rabbi Hugo Gryn in the context of his inclusive approach to inter-faith tolerance, have direct relevance to creativity. For creating does not take place in a vacuum, free of values. Invention is not, *of itself,* good. As human beings we are capable of creating ideas and technologies which destroy others and our environment. Our classrooms and learning spaces need to foster learners' abilities to understand and evaluate the values which underpin their own creativity and that of others. And we need to enable children to reflect critically upon these. As Hugo Gryn's words imply, this means acknowledging the wider environment, and all it contains.

A part of the whole
So, this book has tried to suggest that creativity in classrooms needs to be fostered as a part of a whole. This means that the social context for children needs to form part of the background to creating, whatever the object of creation. All children belong to a community - or more likely, several: for example, their family, their school, their neighbourhood, their friendship groups, their religious or spiritual allegiance (if any), their interest groupings (clubs, activities etc). Creative acts have a potential impact on this wider social context, which may be overlooked in an individualised market-orientated society. As the philosopher, Mary Warnock, has argued (1994), whilst we lock ourselves into a personal identity which puts the individual and their acts of creation first, then we will tend to limit our responsibility for the consequences of our acts to those cases where we can trace our own single and separate cause of action.

We belong to the future
Everything we create today has a relationship with what might be in the future. It is by stimulating creativity and imagination that we can consider the impact of what we do today on what might be.

In dialogue with Rupert Sheldrake, Matthew Fox (1996) talks about our tendency to focus on 'text' rather than 'context'. He is talking about our fragmented relationship with the whole of our environment, in all of its elements - physical, emotional, spiritual, social. His metaphor is appropriate because it signals the intellectual-ist influences on our learning and on our creativity. In fostering children's creativity, we need to remember our relationship as human beings, with our environment. The emotional, physical, spiritual and social dimensions of what we create must become a part of what we value in the classroom. Creativity must be humane, must acknowledge the whole.

In the context of humane creativity, I end with a quotation from George Bernard Shaw. It goes like this.

"You see things that are and say 'why?' But I dream things that never were and say, Why not?"

References
Sheldrake, R., Fox, M.(1996) *Natural Grace: Dialogues on Science and Spirituality,* London: Bloomsbury
Warnock, M. (1994), *Imagination and Time,* Oxford: Blackwell.

APPENDIX ONE
Draft 'Bill of Rights and Responsibilities'

RIGHT TO	RESPONSIBILITY TO

1. Freedom of Expression

Freedom to communicate one's views without fear
Privacy in personal communications
Equal opportunity to express one's views

Tell the truth
Appreciate and bring out the many sides to every issue
See the good in others and express it

2. Freedom of Learning

Freedom of Inquiry
Develop one's knowledge and competence

Be curious, persistent and aware
Learn from past failures and successes
Develop multiple skills
Keep learning and developing

3. Freedom to Act

Choice of projects
Equal opportunity of action
Take individual decisions
Limits to burdens: physical, emotional or caused by the decisions of others

Commit to something worthwhile
Achieve goals
Act with courage and integrity
Respond to the needs of the whole family as well as those of self
Recognise the possible consequences of individual decisions and face up to them if required
Recognise that actions will be seen as inappropriate if they place others in position of vulnerability

4 Freedom to act as member of a team

Freedom of Team Decisions

Recognise the possible consequences of team decisions and face up to them if required
Care for team members
Build the capabilities of every member

5. A Community of Differences

Full membership of the group
A community that cares for your welfare
An ethical group

Neither show nor tolerate bias or prejudice
Balance self-interest against the common good
Work toward worthwhile common vision and values
Find value in diversity

6. Freedom of Own Networks

Freedom of association
Choice of friends
Freedom of choices
Freedom to make and honour commitments

Make commitments wisely
Deliver on one's commitments
Use others' time wisely

7. Group Governance through Participative Democracy

Equal Opportunity to Participate

Listen to others and support their rights
Stand for what one believes in
Use incentives, not mandates, whenever possible
Not manipulate or coerce
Reward service to the whole
Devolve decisions to the lowest possible level

APPENDIX 2

Creating a Declaration and Bill of Rights and Responsibilities[1]

INTRODUCTION

The first assumption I will make is that you will be prepared to act as a champion for this approach within the school. So let me now call you "the initiator".

Basically you will need to initiate a process of cascading dialogue/ conversation/ workshops on these ideas with other members of staff as shown in the figure below. My tips and hints for using the process are linked to the stages of Introduction, Development, Incorporation and Review.

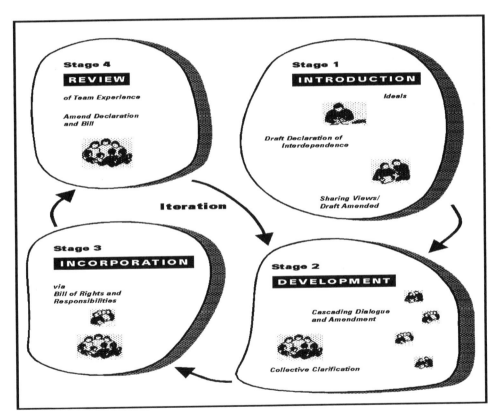

SYSTEMS DESIGN METHODOLOGY WITHIN A TEAM

1 NOTE: The process of creating a Declaration and Bill of Rights and Responsibilities in this appendix has been developed as a model for adaptation to your own school context. The appendix and its annexes should not be reproduced for circulation or distribution without the permission of Gordon Dyer, the author.

This method assumes that there will be a genuine attempt to involve **all** members of the staff group. But there is an issue to consider as the process develops and that is where to draw the boundary around who is involved (including whether and how children in the school could be involved). The principles of system design would make this the widest possible boundary i.e. not just the teaching staff, but teaching assistants, administrators and ancillary staff too. But where the boundary is drawn will be up to the group to evolve as it gains confidence with the process. An important point to bear in mind is that some staff e.g. a cook, or a school keeper, may not be accustomed to having their views sought. They may need full encouragement to join in the process of systems design and to see themselves as a full member of the school staff community.

STAGE 1 - INTRODUCTION

Start by reflecting, yourself, as the initiator, on these questions:

* Will others share your vision that a systems design process within the school would be useful and desirable?

* What core values and beliefs might be identified? Is there a reason for believing that there is a common set of shared values and beliefs?

* Could this be expressed as a future vision of how the staff community should work together?

* Would individuals in the staff community develop personal commitments to achieve that vision?

* Will it be helpful to develop physical documents of this kind, or just to have a draft declaration (and in due course a draft bill of rights and responsibilities) as mechanisms for debate?

Now find at **least one other person** to be positive about these questions. Because of the iterative nature of this process you will almost certainly need to take that person in outline through the next set of questions and possible directions before they will be able to give you a reasonable judgement.

STAGE 2 - DEVELOPMENT OF A POSSIBLE DECLARATION

There are two possible routes from here:

(a) to use the draft as a starting point and then modify it, adapt it as the community wishes,

Or...

(b)　develop a declaration more or less from the beginning

a) Modification Route: To decide whether to adopt or adapt the example provided, ask yourselves:

* Does the draft declaration capture the key issues in terms of the areas of commitment - compassion, diversity, development, and excellence - which ought to be addressed?

* Would these be the right areas of commitment for our school's context? What other domains, if any, might need to be addressed?

* Are there any points within the document, including the introductory statement and concluding statement which we would like to delete, re-express, or add?

* Is the language appropriate?

These questions are suggested as the triggers for conversations and workshops with colleagues. The key point is that everything is up for debate and it is expected that the wording and style of the declaration will evolve as a result until a re-worked draft emerges which is acceptable to colleagues.

b) A New Start: If colleagues are not finding the draft example declaration a useful starting point, then they might wish to take the blank provided at Annex A and develop their own version from scratch.

STAGE 3 - INCORPORATION - DEVELOPMENT OF A POSSIBLE BILL OF RIGHTS AND RESPONSIBILITIES

This should be worked on in largish groups or as a whole community. This is where meaning is going to be added to the ideals within the declaration, and in effect, where 'interdependence' is defined by the group. As with the declaration there are two possible approaches:

(a)　to use the draft bill as a starting point and then modify it, adapt it as the community wishes,

　　　OR

(b)　develop a bill more or less from the beginning

a) Modification Route: To decide whether to adopt or adapt the example provided, ask yourselves the following questions:

* Do the 'areas of freedoms' adequately reflect our school's declaration of interdepend-

ence?

* Should some 'areas of freedom' be deleted, some re-defined or new ones added?

* Are the individual rights and responsibilities within the areas sufficient and adequately expressed?

A possible way to answer these questions is to invite members to give examples of past experience as part of this group:

(i) where being in the group was a positive experience
(ii) where being in the group was a negative experience
(iii) how alternative group behaviour might have avoided a problem.

Such an analysis will help to expose what rights and responsibilities ought to be documented

b) A New Start: If colleagues are not finding the draft example Bill of Rights and Responsibilities a useful starting point, then they might wish to take the blank provided at Annex B and develop their own version from scratch.

STAGE 4 - REVIEW

It will be important to review the group experience every three to six months which could well lead to amendment of the declaration and the bill. True to the principle of systems design the documents could be expected to change as new staff members come into the community and as they are offered the chance to take part in the evolving design.

Appendix 2; Annex A

Template for a Declaration of Independence

The XYZ School Staff Group Declaration of Interdependence - a Statement of Ideals which will continue to evolve. **We the members of the XYZ School Staff Group** *who share .... for one another and for the education and development of the communities in which we live, ... our interdependence.* *DECLARATION OF* *DECLARATION OF*	*DECLARATION OF* *DECLARATION OF* *I realise that I will not always be able to live up to this Declaration of Interdependence. However, all of us, working together through mutual inquiry and conversation, can aontribute to make the Group better, now and in the future, and to make a significant contribution to the larger community.*

Appendix 2; Annex B

Template for a Bill of Rights and Responsibilities

Right to	Responsibility to
1. Freedom of	
2. Freedom of	
3. Freedom to	
4. Freedom to act as	
5. A community of	
6. Freedom of	
7. Group Governance through	

APPENDIX 3

The International Systems Institute

Aims

The International Systems Institute (ISI) is a non-profit, public benefit, scientific and educational agency. ISI is organized as a community of scholars and practitioners and a network of institutions, and has the following objectives:

* Foster individual and collective research in the application of the systems and design sciences;

* Design and develop models, approaches and methods applicable to the analysis, design, development and management of educational and other human activity systems;

* Design and develop resources and programs for systems and design learning;

* Organize and support conferences that provide opportunities for professional development in systems and design applications;

* Develop knowledge-bases in support of the objectives above;

* Develop and publish learning resources, conferences proceedings and monographs that are relavant to the work of the institute;

* Provide resources and assistance to communities engaged in the design of their systems of learning and human development.

Programme and Membership

The program of ISI is carried out by Institute Fellows who pursue the work of ISI in their own organizations as well as in several ISI program areas and research teams.

The ISI is a group currently of some 150 international scholars who are driven by a common belief and value system that the prospect for the future is not promising unless we take the kinds of steps which is encompassed in the systems design approach described in this book; and that this must be started as soon as possible. The membership represents many different cultures, in the Americas: USA, Canada, Mexico, Argentina, Venezuela, in Europe: Belorussia, Estonia, Poland, Hungary, Slovakia, Italy, Austria, Spain, Greece, France, Sweden, Finland, UK, and in the Far East: Japan, Korea, Australia. As educational scholars and practitioners they are also pragmatists, recognising that a huge cultural shift is required which will take a very long time, and that outcomes will be continuously evolutionary. This kind of change has been described by Horiuchi (1994) as social system navigation in that it allows **navigating** towards an Ideal vision, allowing for evolution and adjustments of the Ideal over a very long time-frame.

Over the last 10 years ISI researchers have started to develop a knowledge base and undertake and share research in this new area. The first approaches have been to establish where "small fires" of creative activity are already burning, to encourage others to "light small fires", and to make links to other networks, such as the Creativity in Education community where common ground sponsoring change may be found . The initial strategy is to hope that many small pockets of activity will convert to a wider movement for change.

Origins of ISI and Conversation Meetings

(Taken from: Message to Newcomers— the ISI Story", by Tad frantz in ISI Newsletter, Vol 1, No 1, April 1995. p.3)

ISI was born out of the recognition that academic, scientific and professional conferences seem to offer scant opportunities for colleagues to confer, to converse. Typically,a minority of participants deliver prepared presentations to a reatively passive majority. Except for brief Q & A opportunities, interchange among participants is rarely found on the official schedule. That which does occur is self-organized, informal and wedged into the interstices of the "real" program. Presenting is almost always more prestigious than listening, and some presentations carry greater prestige than others. Traditionally, the prestigious experts disseminate pre-packaged new ideas to the others, who are encouraged to take home and use whatever they find valid or promising.

Such heirarchical knowledge distribution systems greatly constrain us in addressing humanity's most pressing and complex issues, issues about which we are not merely concerned, but also outraged. Of course, at traditional conferences it is well understood that scholars should apporach issues objectively — without emotional involvement.

Bela H. Banathy had a different vision for scholarly gatherings, one which could more fully harness the collective potential of groups. What if all participants were designated presenters and given the opportunity to send prepared papers to the others in advance? And what if extend ed, in-depth, non-hierarchical conversation among them became the program? And what if systems scholars from all over the world focused their conversation together in order to put their expertise actively into the service of humanity worldwide? Bela Banathy established the ISI and inaugurated its first scholarly gatherings at Fuschl Am See, Austria in 1982 to find out. Since then we have called our gatherings "conversations" to distinguish them from traditional conference formats. Participants come to ISI Conversations more to cooperate in making serviceable knowledge than to disperse or gather it, though they are welcome to do both. As Bela Banathy puts it, "We aspire to reap the 'reflecting and creating power' of groups that emerge in the course of disciplined and focused conversations on issues that are important to us and to our society."

The ISI members meet two or three times a year, about 26 sessions each lasting 5 or 6 days have been held in the last 15 years. When groups meet they work in the ***design conversation mode*** and not in the standard conference mode.. this allows us to experience at first hand designing through conversations across cultures. Our conversations emerge around key trigger questions which sustain our effort for about 5 days. The conversation process allows us to explore the diversity of our ideas, beliefs and propositions so that we can then construct a shared meaning of the issue that we have chosen and gain new insight and understanding. In this way we are developing our own competence to conduct such systems and design inquiry that we would need to build our families and communities into learning and designing communities.

The 26 Conversations held to date have been held in a number of European countries. The organisation of a Conversation requires an appropriately sized group of interested people to come forward. The ISI would be happy to sponsor a UK Conversation should demand exist. If you are interested, please contact Gordon Dyer or

Anna Craft, through The Open University:

Gordon Dyer
Deputy Regional Director
Open University Region 6
Cintra House
12 Hills Road
Cambridge
CB2 1PF

Anna Craft
The Open University School of Education
Walton Hall
Milton Keynes
MK7 6AA

Research outlets

The ISI publishes through a number of Journals including *Systems Research*, and *Systems Practice, Educational Technology, Educational Horizons, World Futures*, and the Japanese journal, *Review of Administration and Informatics*. Included in the published work, e.g. this book, are some suggestions for methodology for systems design. Such metholodolgy would best be described as proto-methodology in that it indicates the main areas in a map of design journey, e.g. the space of "image creation". Such milestones do not give us an indication of how far we have to go, but some insights into what further questions we might need to ask.. These questions often lead to the triggers for conversations and published work. Some of the work has some very interesting titles, which include phrases .. designing design conversations... getting ready for designing design conversations. One of the projects at the moment is designing a bi-lingual design conversation which is to be held in Japan in May 1997.. where Japanese is the primary language. The aspiration that ISI has to cascade systems design to other, non-Western cultures has taken its first step.

Organisational Context

The main international point of contact for the ISI is:

The ISI International Office
25781 Morse Drive
Carmel, CA 93923
U.S.A.

Web Site

Further details can be found at the ISI Web site:

www.clark.net/pub/nhp/isi